Seeing
Gray
in a World of
Black and White

Praise for Seeing Gray in a World of Black and White

"While reality is presented in church and our culture these days as black or white, either/or, left or right, conservative or liberal, Adam Hamilton skillfully, carefully, and faithfully helps us see the wisdom and humble way of gray. In religious and scientific questions, in the hot buttons in most denominations today (like abortion and homosexuality), in an approach to reading the Scriptures, and more, he shows 'a more excellent,' third alternative to the extreme polar opposites we assume are the only ones available to us. I highly recommend that all United Methodists read this important book to help us find the radical center that combines social and personal holiness again."
—Sally Dyck, Resident Bishop Minnesota Area, The United Methodist Church

"I loved this book! Hamilton offers a solidly biblical and immensely reasonable middle ground on virtually every major issue that presently divides our country as well as the church. Of course, few will agree with every one of Hamilton's own conclusions. But everyone who reads this wonderfully written book will be positively impacted by its humble, Christlike style. In our polarized climate, this is exactly what we need!"
—Gregory A. Boyd, Princeton Seminary; Senior Pastor of Woodland Hills Church, Maplewood, Minn.

"Adam Hamilton invites us to soulful gray space between polarities, glorious gray space that is holy, mysterious, complex, and true. Let us find within our spirits the courage and humility to live and learn in this faithful space, to see gray, to discern a more excellent way."
—Hope Morgan Ward, Resident Bishop, Mississippi Annual Conference, The United Methodist Church

"Adam is a breath of fresh air. True to Scripture but no simple 'god in a box' formulas for the church to be found in these pages."
—Mike Slaughter

Continued on page 246.

To David,
Blessings!
Adam Hamilton

Adam Hamilton

Seeing

Gray

in a World of
Black and White

Thoughts on Religion,
Morality, and Politics

Abingdon Press
Nashville

SEEING GRAY IN A WORLD OF BLACK AND WHITE
THOUGHTS ON RELIGION, MORALITY, AND POLITICS

Copyright © 2008 by Abingdon Press

This book is printed on acid-free paper.

Library of Congress Cataloging-in-Publication Data

Hamilton, Adam, 1964–
    Seeing gray in a world of black and white : thoughts on religion, morality, and politics / Adam Hamilton.
        p. cm.
    ISBN 978-0-687-64969-3 (binding: hardback with a dust jacket : alk. paper)
    1. United States—Church history—21st century. 2. Christianity—United States.
    3. Christianity and culture—United States. 4. Christianity and politics—United States.
    I. Title.

    BR526.H245 2008
    261.0973—dc22

                                                                                    2008002409

Scripture quotations, unless otherwise noted, are from the New Revised Standard Version of the Bible, copyright 1989, Division of Christian Education of the National Council of the Churches of Christ in the United States of America. Used by permission. All rights reserved.

Scripture marked KJV is from the King James or Authorized Version of the Bible.

Scripture marked NIV is taken from the Holy Bible, NEW INTERNATIONAL VERSION®. Copyright © 1973, 1978, 1984 by International Bible Society. All rights reserved throughout the world. Used by permission of International Bible Society.

10 11 12 13 14 15 16 17—10 9 8 7 6 5
MANUFACTURED IN THE UNITED STATES OF AMERICA

To My Daughters, Danielle and Rebecca

Contents

Contents

Foreword

Jim Wallis

As I travel around the country, I meet a new generation of pastors and leaders who are creating new conversation about the relation between personal faith and social justice. They and their churches are catching fire with the gospel, and are applying the message and mission of the kingdom of God to a hurting humanity. Their vision cannot easily be put into the old categories of liberal or conservative, left or right, social gospel or fundamentalist. They are instead challenging the categories themselves.

One of these leaders is Adam Hamilton, founding pastor of the United Methodist Church of the Resurrection. I had been hearing about Adam Hamilton for a while when a mutual friend put us in touch with each other. I was told that his church is the largest Methodist church in the country, a sign that not all mainline Protestant churches are in decline. We have now had a few conversations, and I read his new book, discovering that we have much in common. In both faith and politics, Hamilton is seeking to forge a new path that transcends the extremes of our polarized and paralyzed political culture and our divided church. In this book, he writes of combining "a passionate evangelistic zeal coupled with a belief that the gospel had to be lived in social ministry to a broken world."

The people I meet across the country are yearning for what I call a "moral center" to our public life and political discourse, with a fundamental emphasis on the common good. But this is not just another argument for more centrist politics, so much in vogue these days. The mushy political middle isn't the answer and a vague and compromising centrism that merely splits the difference on whatever the current political spectrum happens to be at the moment isn't particularly attractive.

Rather, those I meet across the nation and around the world want to actually respond to the moral choices and challenges that lie just beneath our political debates. They don't want to just go "left" or "right," but deeper. Seeking to find the moral ground on which a new consensus can be built and better decisions made is much more appealing than a weak and soulless centrism. More and more people want to see a new common-good politics and bridge-building church.

The moral center also appeals to the center of people's lives, which current political and religious options often do not. What are the real and practical issues that affect people's daily experience and relate to what is actually going on in their everyday decisions, challenges, and choices? What is at the center of people's lives and what appeals to their most basic moral concerns and values? It's time to create a new spiritual and political language, from a moral center, that focuses on the pressing moral questions we face today.

Adam Hamilton calls this the "radical center," a concept that culminates a series of very thoughtful essays on a variety of topics from how to heal the bitter debates raging in our churches, the battle over the Bible, religion and science, heaven and hell, faith and doubt, situation ethics, homosexuality, abortion, war, how Christians should choose a president, and a new vision for America, among other themes.

Conservatives have been right about the importance of culture and values and the necessity of personal responsibility; but they have been morally compromised by favoring the rich over the poor and middle classes and by conforming to American nationalism and militarism. Liberals have been right to talk about social responsibility and the need for government to ensure fairness and opportunity and a more level playing field; but they have often failed to affirm the importance of fundamental moral values in our national life, which could be done without compromising their values of democracy and pluralism.

As the limitations of the current political options have become more apparent and as their ideological rigidity blocks social cooperation and political solutions, I have become ever more convinced of the need for another way. And one seems to be emerging. We see a new kind of politics growing around the country. It is socially "conservative" or traditional on matters of personal behavior and responsibility, rooted in strong moral values that include the sanctity of human life, and deeply committed to the crucial bonds of family. At the same time, it is also strongly populist with regard to economic fairness and justice, quite communitarian in its sense of social responsibility, deeply committed to environmental care, and increasingly skeptical of war in its stance toward foreign policy. At the heart of this new (and very old) option is the integral link between personal ethics and social justice, and the refusal to separate the two.

Perhaps it is time to move beyond the old exclusive categories of liberalism and conservatism. Maybe what we need is a new paradigm altogether—we might call it *the conservative radical*. To be conservative means to be rooted—in a tradition, in faith, in core values. To be radical also means to be rooted (*radical* comes from the Latin word *radix*, meaning "root"), which gives one a consistent perspective on the world. So these two—radical and conservative—may not be contradictory but in fact deeply complementary.

What we need most are people rooted in "conservative" values and commitments but willing to be "radical" enough to apply those very values in the real world. If we are to preserve the values (a conservative goal) of equality and justice, for example, they require radical application to the needs of a broken world (a liberal goal). Dorothy Day of the Catholic Worker Movement was a conservative radical—applying the values of her faith to life. It has been said that "she loved the truth enough to live it." So were Mother Teresa, Martin Luther King, Jr., and Dietrich Bonhoeffer—they were all rooted in conservative traditions that made them radicals in the world.

Ultimately, we are known and judged by what we say yes to and what we say no to. We say yes in accordance with the conservative values that root us; then, say a radical no when those same values require it. A conservative radical doesn't fall neatly into any of our modern political categories and options but could help transform them all. And that might lead us to some real solutions, and perhaps even bring a measure of peace to a political culture that is still at war.

In the midst of thinking about all this and preparing my own book on these themes, also to be published this year, I met Adam Hamilton and read his book, *Seeing Gray in a World of Black and White*. I found it refreshing, creative, insightful and, to use a biblical description, prophetic. It offers the new approach and ethic of the "both/and," instead of the old and tired "either/or." Adam is the kind of "conservative radical" that I have been hoping for, and his notion of the "radical center" is a place that more and more people would like to call home. Reading this book was an encouragement to me and I trust it will also be to you.

Introduction
Are Jerry Falwell and John Shelby Spong Our Only Options?

It was 1991 and I was getting ready for work while watching *Good Morning America*. Just before a commercial, host Charles Gibson announced that when he returned he'd be joined by two clergy, the Reverend Jerry Falwell, the pastor of Thomas Road Baptist Church, and Bishop John Shelby Spong, Episcopal bishop of Newark, New Jersey. Falwell had founded the Moral Majority and was known as America's most outspoken fundamentalist. Spong had just written a book entitled *Rescuing the Bible from Fundamentalism*, and he was quickly gaining a reputation as America's most outspoken liberal Christian.

Jerry Falwell believed that the Bible was to be taken literally, and that wherever the modern world conflicted with the Bible, the modern world was wrong. John Shelby Spong noted that neither he, nor many of the people he knew, could bend their minds into first-century pretzels any more, and thus he could

> I found myself thinking,
>
> "These two cannot be
>
> our only options
>
> for being Christian!"

not accept a literal reading of Scripture. He noted that there were many places where the Bible was simply in error. Theologically, sociologically, and politically they were diametrically opposed. In listening to them, I found places where I sympathized with Spong, and others where I sympathized with Falwell. But by the time their "conversation" was over I found myself thinking, "These two cannot be our only options for being Christian!"

The truth is, most Christians find themselves somewhere in between these two extremes. Most evangelicals found Falwell too conservative long before his comments following 9/11 that the ACLU, abortionists, and gays and lesbians had to "take a lot of the blame for this" (a statement he retracted a day later with an apology). Most liberals are unwilling to follow Spong as he discards nearly all of the historic doctrines of the Christian faith. These two men represented a kind of black-and-white world, Falwell's yin to Spong's yang. Falwell's kind of Christianity emerged as a reaction to late nineteenth-century modernism. Spong's liberalism was a reaction to Falwell's kind of late twentieth-century fundamentalism.

The history of ideas and movements within Christianity has often been reactive, like the swinging of a pendulum. Using the language of Newton's Third Law of Motion, major movements within Chrisitanity have too often reflected the fact that "for every action there is an equal and opposite reaction." The Reformation was a reaction to Catholicism's shortcomings in the fifteenth and sixteenth centuries. Yet in its more radical expressions the pendulum swung too far, making claims and pursuing practices that, in essence, threw the proverbial baby out with the bathwater. Likewise fundamentalism might be seen as an "equal and opposite" reaction to "modernism"—a pendulum that swung as far to the right as modernism or liberalism at its most radical had swung to the left.

> Fundamentalism might be seen as an "equal and opposite" reaction to "modernism"— a pendulum that swung as far to the right as modernism or liberalism at its most radical had swung to the left.

Falwell and Spong represent the poles or extremes of the last quarter century. The extremes have clear views on every subject, and those views are black and white enough to enable one to articulate them in brief sound bites. This is why people like Falwell and Spong are often called upon for comment by the media. Unfortunately, when the people representing the Christian community are Jerry Falwell or Pat Robertson on the one side, and John Shelby Spong on the other, you end up with a wide gulf in between with no one articulating a middle way.

It seems to me that increasingly there are large swaths of the Christian population who are yearning for a middle way. There are self-described evangelicals who are embracing elements of the social gospel and who are open to insights from historical critical methods of biblical study. There are self-described liberal Christians who are embracing elements of the evangelical gospel, who are speaking of their "personal relationship with Jesus Christ," and who are learning to give evangelistic altar calls while still championing social justice. And, perhaps exemplifying this trend, there are those who describe their faith as "emergent" or "postmodern" and who yearn for a "generous orthodoxy."

Increasingly there are large swaths of the population yearning for a middle way.

As many Christians are drawn to a centered or balanced faith, there is an increasing frustration with the role that Christianity has played in the culture wars. Too often faith has been used by Christian leaders and politicians to further a particular political party or political agenda. And in the minds of many nonreligious people in America, Christianity is not associated with love or grace or justice, but with a particular view of homosexuality, or a particular stance on abortion, or a seemingly absurd and anti-intellectual view of human origins. Christianity has become a wedge that drives people from Christ, rather than drawing them to him. And Christians have, in their political involvement, acted to divide our nation rather than serve as the balm that can heal it.

There are a growing number of Christians who believe the gospel calls us to be healers and bridge builders, not dividers. There are new calls to civility in how Christians dialogue and debate ethical and political issues. And there are many Christians who are coming to see that even on the important ethical issues of our time there may be a need for a different approach than has been taken in the last thirty years.

This book is my attempt at laying out one Christian's view of a Christianity of the *via media* or middle way between the extremes. It is not a systematic theology or textbook on ethics. It is a series of essays on various topics meant to serve as a constructive proposition—an invitation for you to think about the various topics to see if they make sense to you. You'll agree with some and disagree with others. I suspect that as time goes by, my own views will change on some of these topics. But this is a place to start the discussion on what a Christianity of the middle way might look like.

I've organized the essays into three parts. The first introduces the idea of seeing gray in a world of black and white and the characteristics of a Christianity of the middle way. The second part turns to the issue of the Bible, oft-debated questions concerning evolution, the fate of non-Christians, and the problem of suffering, before ending with a look at Christian spirituality. The third part turns to issues of ethics and politics. Here we'll consider the controversial topics of abortion, homosexuality, and war before turning to a couple of chapters that seek to look at the relationship between faith and politics.

My own approach to controversial issues, first laid out in my book, *Confronting the Controversies* (Abingdon Press, 2001, 2005), is that any issue about which thinking Christians disagree likely has important truth on each side of the debate. The key is to listen to both sides and look for ways to integrate the legitimate concerns of each side, often forging a new way forward, or at least plowing forward while taking seriously the views of the other. This willingness to listen to those with whom we disagree, and to take seriously their legitimate concerns, is critical for people of all religions and nationalities. Until we can learn to do that, there will be no hope for resolving the culture wars here at home, nor the broader international conflicts that threaten our world.

I believe that Christianity is in need of a new reformation. The fundamentalism of the last century is waning. And the liberalism of the last fifty years has jettisoned too much of the historic Christian gospel to take its place. Christianity's next reformation will strike a middle path between Jerry Falwell and John Shelby Spong. It will draw upon what is best in both fundamentalism and liberalism by holding together the evangelical and social gospels, by combining a love of Scripture with a willingness to see both its humanity as well as its divinity, and by coupling a passionate desire to follow Jesus Christ with a reclamation of his heart toward those whom religious people have often rejected. This reformation will be led by people who are able to see the gray in a world of black and white.

Part I
Seeing the Gray
in a
Black-and-White World

One
Are You Liberal or Conservative?

> *The division of the world into "liberal" and "conservative" . . .*
> *is one of the really restricting developments that has ever happened*
> *to us. . . . It has to be, we are told, either this way or that. Such a*
> *view makes things very simple, I suppose. But it also reduces our*
> *minds to utter fuzziness. We are required to define everything as ei-*
> *ther liberal or conservative even when the two allowable terms of*
> *definition are not adequate to explain the reality that they are in-*
> *tended to describe.*
> —Fr. James V. Schall, S.J. [1]

I came to faith in Christ as a teenager. I'd been away from church for years when someone invited me to a small Pentecostal church. While it was the girls in the church who inspired me to return after my first visit, I also found myself drawn to the passionate faith of the people in that congregation. It was in reading the Bible, though, that I actually decided to follow Jesus Christ, inviting Jesus Christ to be my Savior and Lord. I was fourteen.

When I was sixteen I felt God calling me to be a pastor. Upon graduating from high school, I began attending Oral Roberts University (ORU) where I would eventually earn my bachelor's degree in pastoral ministry. I entered ORU as a Pentecostal with very conservative and fundamentalist views. While ORU was certainly no bastion of liberalism, it was there that I found myself stretched and many of my fundamentalist assumptions challenged.

I loved the passion of the Pentecostal church I attended, and I did not waver in my desire to be a follower of Jesus, but I had lots of questions about faith, the Scriptures, and the "fundamental truths" I had been taught. I began reading the minor prophets and

3

then the Gospels once again, and I began to see that God's call was not simply to tell others the good news, or even only that we have a "personal relationship" with him (as life-giving as this is). He also wanted us to do justice, to be concerned for the poor, and to provide help to those in need.

I left the Pentecostal church in college, and began searching for a new spiritual home. I did not want to jettison what I felt was good in my Pentecostal experience—the personal relationship with Jesus Christ, a love of the Scriptures, and an emphasis on the work of the Holy Spirit. But I yearned for a church that would link these with a passion for justice, and where the intellect was valued as much as the heart.

In the end my search led me to John Wesley, the eighteenth-century founder of the Methodist movement. His movement, Methodism, was born out of the theological conflicts that preceded him, and rather than finding himself drawn to the extremes, Wesley drew from them all as he articulated a gospel of the middle way. I joined The United Methodist Church when I was nineteen.

Joining The United Methodist Church meant that I would now need to attend graduate school in order to be ordained. I was encouraged to attend a conservative seminary, but I felt that it was important to be exposed to the theological and biblical interpretations of a bit more liberal seminary. I opted for Perkins School of Theology at Southern Methodist University. Its place on the theological spectrum may have been slightly left of center, but relative to Oral Roberts it was clearly "liberal."

What I found by virtue of having attended a somewhat conservative college and a somewhat liberal seminary was an opportunity to listen to and explore the truth found on both sides of the theological divide. In the end I came to appreciate both theological liberals and conservatives. Both liberals and conservatives had important characteristics and theological positions that I found compelling. I began to wonder, "Are these my only choices? Am I either a liberal or a conservative? Or is there something in between?"

In the same way, an increasing number of Christians today are finding it difficult to identify with either side of this theological

4

divide. They are not certain how to answer the question, "Are you liberal or conservative?"

A "liberal" pastor I know opposes abortion, but favors allowing homosexuals to enter into marriage-like covenants. He has a heart for evangelism and takes great joy in inviting people to follow Jesus Christ as their Lord and Savior *and* he protested the war in Iraq when most of the nation was in favor of it. He even gives "altar calls" from time to time. This pastor would never consider voting for a Republican for president.

A "conservative" pastor I know told me he did not see how he could be a Christian and not be liberal on such issues as the environment and poverty, and he favors raising taxes to address these concerns. He's opened medical clinics for low-income people and has hosted interfaith services in his "conservative" church. And this same pastor all but endorsed George W. Bush for president in the 2004 election. Some have left his church because he was "too liberal," though he embraces all of the theological beliefs of early fundamentalism. As these examples illustrate, even those who use the labels of liberal and conservative to describe themselves don't always neatly fit into these camps.

What is true of these pastors is increasingly true of Christians in general in the United States. The results of a 2006 Pew Forum study of more than 2,000 Americans, entitled "Pragmatic Americans Liberal and Conservative on Social Issues," captures well the fact that a large number of Americans, regardless of the particular label they tend to claim for themselves, already see the world as a bit more gray than their labels would suppose. Researchers found that "Americans cannot be easily characterized as conservative or liberal." [2]

When people ask me, "Are you liberal or conservative?" my answer is usually, "Yes!" My answer is yes for several reasons. First, I see both liberal and conservative as two parts of a whole. When we say that someone is liberal with their giving, we mean that he or she is generous. I want to be liberal in that sense of the word! If *liberal* is defined as "favoring reform," that, too, captures my heart as a Protestant, because it recalls one of the important

> If liberal is defined as "favoring reform," that, too, captures my heart as a Protestant, because it recalls one of the important Reformation slogans, *ecclesia reformata, semper reformanda:* "the church reformed, always reforming."

Reformation slogans, *ecclesia reformata, semper reformanda:* "the church reformed, always reforming." If *liberal* is a synonym for "broad-minded" or "open-minded" then yes, I wish to be a liberal!

Yet if "conservative" means holding on to what is good from the past, and being cautious in embracing change simply for the sake of change, then mark me conservative! If being conservative within the Christian community means retaining the historic doctrines of the Christian faith as articulated in the creeds, then I am conservative. If conservative means, as the Latin, *conservare* does, guarding, keeping, or observing (presumably the treasures of the past), then, at least with regard to many things, I must be conservative.

On the other hand, if *liberal* means holding to the absolute right of individuals to do whatever they choose, or if *conservative* means simply seeking to maintain the status quo, I could not be defined as either liberal or conservative!

I might also respond to the person who asks me "are you liberal or conservative?" by noting, "It depends on who is asking." *Liberal* and *conservative* are relative terms and all but the most extreme among us are liberal relative to some people and conservative relative to others.

One of Kansas's most famous pastors is a man named Fred Phelps of Westboro Baptist Church, a congregation of around one hundred members. Phelps and the members of his church travel across the country to protest at a number of

> If "conservative" means holding on to what is good from the past, and being cautious in embracing change simply for the sake of change, then mark me conservative!

6

events, including the funerals of homosexuals and military personnel. Their signs carry slogans indicating their belief in God's judgment on homosexual persons, and on American society for tolerating homosexuality (for more about the group's beliefs, visit their website: www.god hatesfags.com). In 2007, the group protested at the funeral of perhaps the most famous "conservative" pastor in America at the time: the Reverend Dr. Jerry Falwell. The conclusion I have reached about this protest is that, despite the fact that Falwell was seen by most as a staunch conservative, he was "liberal" from Phelps's perspective, and "soft" on homosexuality! Liberal and conservative are relative terms—we're all more liberal than someone, and more conservative than someone else.

> *Liberal* and *conservative* are relative terms and all but the most extreme among us are liberal relative to some people and conservative relative to others.

Even Fred Phelps isn't so easily confined to a box. For two decades following his graduation from law school Phelps was a civil rights lawyer waging legal battles on behalf of African Americans as he opposed discrimination. He was recognized for these efforts by the NAACP in the 1980s, before he became known for his virulent antihomosexual positions. We human beings are an odd and sometimes confused lot.

Conservative and *liberal*, then, are both terms that might apply to most of us. And, in the best sense of these words, most of us likely recognize the value of conserving some things, and being cautious in simply accepting change for change's sake. And we would also recognize the value of being broad-minded, generous, and willing to embrace reform or change when such change is deemed necessary. Many of us are liberal on some issues and conservative on others. Someone more conservative than you thinks of

> *Conservative* and *liberal*, then, are terms that might both apply to most of us.

you as a liberal; likewise, your liberal neighbor considers you a conservative.

Even our most basic of ways of categorizing people in our society—left/right, liberal/conservative—point us to the truth that the world is not always black and white, and more often than not, we find ourselves somewhere in the gray between the two.

In the next few chapters in this section I'd like to point out some basic commands that Jesus offers his followers that, if followed, would bring an end to Christians serving as the wedge in America's culture wars. Following these commands of Jesus would allow us instead to be bridge builders, peacemakers, and healers. But following these commands is only possible when we've begun to recognize that the world is not always black and white, and when we've begun to appreciate its many shades of gray.

Notes

1. "On Being Neither Liberal nor Conservative," www.ignatiusinsight.com/features2005/schall_libcons_may05.asp.
2. See www.pewforum.org/docs/index.php?DocID=150.

Two
Straining Gnats

"You blind guides! You strain out a gnat but swallow a camel!"
—*Matthew 23:24*

Among the struggles we have as human beings is our tendency to "major in the minors." We describe this in a host of ways: We "can't see the forest for the trees." We "win the battle and lose the war." We struggle to "keep the main thing the main thing." We make "a mountain out of a molehill." While this is a universal affliction of all human beings, religious people excel at it.

Jesus criticized the religious leaders of his day for this when he said,

> Our desire for certainty, our need to be right, and our tendency to miss the point have conspired to keep Christians from experiencing unity, and instead have led to endless divisions within the Christian faith.

> "Woe to you, scribes and Pharisees, hypocrites! For you tithe mint, dill, and cummin, and have neglected the weightier matters of the law: justice and mercy and faith. It is these you ought to have practiced without neglecting the others. You blind guides! You strain out a gnat but swallow a camel!" (Matthew 23:23-24)

As he was facing his own death, Jesus prayed for unity among his followers, knowing, no doubt, that they would struggle with their own tendency to strain gnats, argue endlessly over matters of doctrine, and be forever dividing over mint, dill and cumin—Jesus' metaphor for focusing on the irrelevant details (John 17:20-24).

Our desire for certainty, our need to be right, and our tendency to miss the point have conspired to keep Christians from experiencing unity, and instead have led to endless divisions within the Christian faith. In America alone there are over two thousand different Christian denominations and tens of thousands of churches that are independent and nondenominational churches. Though all claim to be followers of Jesus, most have divided over matters of doctrine or ways of practicing their faith. Each feels that their doctrine and practice is more faithful than the others.

In 2007 a document released by the Vatican made front-page news around the world. The document, which intended to clarify the Roman Catholic Church's position on non-Catholic churches, noted that non-Catholic churches are wounded or defective and that Protestant churches are not truly "churches" in the technical sense of the word. What is it that makes Protestant and Orthodox churches—more than 1 billion of the world's Christians—"defective" or "wounded"? The fact that these other Christians do not accept the authority of the pope, and that many do not accept the idea of apostolic succession or the Catholic view of the sacrament of Holy Communion (the Eucharist).

At the time these comments were made, I wrote the following reflections. They capture how "seeing gray" might help different churches and denominations better understand and relate to one another.

From One "Defective" Christian to Another

The world was recently reminded of one of the tragic realities of contemporary Christianity: Christians claim to follow Jesus, the man who chastised religious leaders for their proficiency at missing the point, became frustrated by the religiosity that excluded and judged deficient broad swaths of the populace in first-century Judea, and made it clear that prostitutes and sinners were welcome in the kingdom of God. Nonetheless, these same Christians

> Jesus, the man who chastised religious leaders for their proficiency at missing the point, became frustrated by the religiosity that excluded and judged deficient broad swaths of the populace in first-century Judea, and made it clear that prostitutes and sinners were welcome in the kingdom of God. Nonetheless, these same Christians excel at focusing on theological minutiae while excluding their fellow-followers of Jesus, judging others' faith and churches to be defective.

excel at focusing on theological minutiae while excluding their fellow-followers of Jesus, judging others' faith and churches to be defective.

While the Vatican is at the center of the current flap, it is not alone in holding such views. One Orthodox priest told me that he was not certain what the fate of the world's 1.9 billion Catholics and Protestants would be on the Day of Judgment. Conversely, there are millions of Protestants who do not believe that the world's 1.1 billion Catholics and 300 million Orthodox are authentically Christian. Then there are the internecine battles among Protestants, many of whom believe most of their fellow Protestants are also defective and deficient in their faith.

In hearing these kinds of conversations, I am reminded of my two daughters, age seventeen and twenty-one. They could not be more different from each other. Their personalities and tastes in clothing, music, food, and boys are worlds apart. Even the churches they are drawn to differ. Though I am a United Methodist pastor, my older daughter, at least while away at college, prefers the rich liturgy of the Episcopal Church to standard Methodist fare. And my younger daughter prefers the "emergent" and "edgy" worship of a church whose pastor wears blue jeans and T-shirts and whose members have piercings and tattoos.

When my daughters were younger they would each say to the other, "Dad loves me more than you." But the truth is, for all their differences, I love them both with the same intensity—I love them so much it hurts sometimes—and so much that I would give my life for them. I delight in their differences. I love their unique characteristics and their diverse ways of seeing the world. And I believe my feelings about my daughters are a reflection of how Jesus sees his followers in their various churches.

I love my Roman Catholic friends, and my faith is richer for listening to them share their experience of the eucharistic mystery and the traditions of their church. I have a deep respect for my Orthodox neighbors and feel a sense of mystery and awe when I worship amid the aroma of incense in their church. I love my Southern Baptist colleagues, whose love of the Scriptures and preaching of conversion have left their mark on me. And my Pentecostal friends have reminded me that the Holy Spirit continues to work in unexpected ways I can't control. While I'm drawn to The United Methodist Church's attempt to hold together the evangelical and social gospels, and to stand in the center of the theological spectrum as a bridge between the left and the right, I don't believe all Christians should be United Methodists. In fact, I think Christianity would be the poorer if they were.

The truth is that all of the branches in this tree called Christianity are a bit defective. But each adds to the beauty of the whole. What a tragedy if we were to cut off all but one of the limbs. But what riches are to be found if we can humbly listen and learn from one another, appreciating our differences, while together seeking to follow Jesus Christ.[1]

How often the Christian church's ability to accomplish good is diminished by our infighting. What if all 224 million Christians in America were actually working together to shape a nation that looks like Jesus' vision of the kingdom of God, where poverty does not exist, where people practice justice, where love of neighbor is universally practiced? But this will never happen. We are too busy "straining gnats."

Our quest for truth, certainty, purity of doctrine, and our tendency to label others who don't agree with us, to separate from them and to demonize them, lead us back to black-and-white, either/or thinking. I am right and you are wrong. I am faithful and you are unfaithful. I am whole and you are wounded or defective. We have "all the gospel," and you do not.

I am not suggesting that we could ever return to a time when all Christians are "of one accord" as was seen on the day of Pentecost in the early church. Even then the unity didn't last for long. But the hope for the future of Christianity will be found, in part, in our willingness to accept that no one of us has all of the truth. We must be able to see the value in another's position, practice, and doctrine. And while we may hold fast to our convictions, we must be willing to accept that someone else could be correct, and we could be in error, or we both might be partially correct. Alternatively, we might simply be willing to say, "This issue is not worth dividing over." This sentiment has been captured in the well-known quotation, "In essentials, unity; in doubtful matters, liberty; in all things, charity." [2]

> But the hope for the future of Christianity will be found, in part, in our willingness to accept that no one of us has all of the truth. We must be able to see the value in another's position, practice, and doctrine.

The challenge, of course, comes in deciding what constitutes an essential matter, and what is a doubtful or nonessential matter. For some Christians a particular view of the Bible's inspiration and authority is an essential. For others it is nonessential. For some the mode of baptism is an essential, for others it is a nonessential. The early Christians wrestled with this, and their answers were faith statements captured in the creeds of the church, statements that were meant to summarize what the church believed. These were never comprehensive statements, but an attempt to capture the most important theological issues.

Ultimately, what is needed is humility. I appreciate the statement of Sir John Templeton: "Humility is a gateway to greater understanding and open[s] the doors to progress."[3] Templeton is known for being the proponent of what he calls, "the humble approach" to both science and religion. Humility is essential to Christian faith. And that humility should be rooted in our expanding awareness of how small we are and how truly great God is.

At one point in my Christian journey I was absolutely persuaded that anyone who did not believe just as I did about certain issues was not only wrong but quite possibly not truly Christian. Yet later I came to think about those issues very differently myself. I think back on some of the religious arguments I had with others in the early years of my faith. Enough experiences discovering I had been wrong have led me to a bit of humility when it comes to my convictions. I believe them to be true, but I am willing to allow that, in the words of the Apostle Paul, "we see through a mirror dimly," and therefore, I may be wrong.

I have always had a fascination with the stars. When I am in danger of thinking I've got God and life figured out, I step outside on a dark night and look up. Contemplating the cosmos is meant to lead us to the same conclusion the psalmist had when he wrote,

> When I look at your heavens, the work of your fingers,
>   the moon and the stars that you have established;
> what are human beings that you are mindful of them?
> (Psalm 8:3-4a)

Terence Dickinson, in his wonderful book *The Universe and Beyond,* helps us put our lives, thoughts, and place in the universe in perspective when he notes that if we could travel at the speed of light (186,000 miles per second), it would take us 80,000 years just to cross our own Milky Way galaxy. Our galaxy alone contains over 200 billion stars like our sun. Once leaving our galaxy, traveling at 186,000 miles per second, it would take us 42,000 years just to get to the next closest galaxy from the center of our own.[4] There are more than 100 billion galaxies in the universe. It would take us 156 billion years, traveling at the speed of light, to cross the entire universe.[5] This is a vast universe! God stands outside of, and his presence permeates, the entire universe. God is at work in the ongoing creation of new planets, stars, and galaxies. God rules over the vastness of the universe, and sustains it by his power. Our galaxy is but one small part of God's cosmos, and our planet is but one speck in our galaxy, and each of us is but one of six billion people living in this moment in time. As one subatomic particle is to my entire body, so I am to the entire cosmos.

This knowledge, too, should lead us to a heavy dose of humility when it comes to our pronouncements about God and our own self-importance. Each of us possesses approximately three pounds of gray matter within our skull, most of which we don't ever use. Do we really believe that we are capable of understanding the mysteries of God or knowing fully the mind of God? Yes, the Bible helps us know the mind of God, but even here the communication of divine knowledge is limited by language, the ability of the biblical authors to understand and convey God's will and ways, and our ability to comprehend this knowledge and to rightly interpret the Scriptures. Again with the psalmist we might say, "Such knowledge is too wonderful for me; it is so high that I cannot attain it" (Psalm 139:6).

Many are persuaded that when the third commandment prohibits us from "taking God's name in vain" it is not referring

> Each of us possesses approximately three pounds of gray matter within our skull, most of which we don't ever use. Do we really believe that we are capable of understanding the mysteries of God or knowing fully the mind of God?

15

to swearing. Instead it is a call to humility and caution in inappropriately invoking or misusing God's name. This is captured in the New Revised Standard Version of this commandment: "You shall not make wrongful use of the name of the LORD your God, for the LORD will not acquit anyone who misuses his name" (Exodus 20:7). There are many ways we might misuse God's name, but among these is making statements about God that God himself would reject. I believe the terrorists who invoke God's name before killing innocent people is one clear example. But so, too, are the many things pastors and preachers say about God, with utter confidence, but which God might find the antithesis of his heart and character.

In 1952, J. B. Phillips wrote a brief book whose content is helpful, but whose title alone led me to buy it: *Your God Is Too Small.* Phillips warns against a faith that makes God to be small and inadequate. I fear that today the Christian church (along with every other religion) is often guilty of worshiping a small God whose mystery we think we've nailed down in our black-and-white theology such that we can proclaim that only our church or denomination fully understands the mind and will of God. I believe that conservatives and liberals alike are often guilty of worshiping, following, and making pronouncements on behalf of a God who is far too small.

When I was in college a preacher came to town leading a kind of revival for young adults. He preached on the sin of listening to rock-and-roll music. He called us to take all of our rock albums and throw them away because it was the devil's music and God was displeased by this music. I wanted to please God. I didn't want to give the devil any room to work in my life, so I decided to go home that night and discard my album collection. My favorite group as I was growing up in the 1970s was the Beatles. Though they had broken up in 1970, when I was six, I loved their music and had quite a collection of original Beatles LPs I had begun collecting when I was nine. I went home to my apartment that evening, carried my albums to the dumpster, and threw them in. Actually, before tossing them I broke each one in half so that no one could find them in the dumpster, take them back to his or her apartment and be "led astray by the devil" as I may have been!

I believe there are musical expressions that we as Christians should not listen to: music whose lyrics are degrading to women, promote violence, and glamorize drug use. But the music I put in the dumpster that night was "She loves you, yeah, yeah, yeah!" And on the day the preacher was telling me that God wanted me to throw away my Beatles albums thirty-two thousand people around the world died of starvation and malnutrition-related diseases! We were straining gnats while people were dying of hunger!

Are you, or is your church, ever guilty of straining gnats? Is your God "too small"? Gray calls us to humility, and to worship a God that is bigger than we can begin to fully comprehend.

Notes

1. I tried to model this way of seeing the various Christian churches in my book, *Christianity's Family Tree* (Abingdon Press, 2007). In it I invited readers to listen and learn from eight different traditions within the Christian faith (Orthodoxy, Catholicism, Lutheranism, Presbyterianism, Anglicanism, the Baptist traditions, Pentecostalism and Methodism).
2. This quote is variously attributed to St. Augustine, John Wesley, or, most likely, seventeenth-century–Lutheran Rupertus Melendius. See www.ccat.sas.upenn.edu/jod/augustine/quote.html.
3. See www.templeton.org/science_and_religion/humbleapproach.asp.
4. Canis Major is our closest galactic neighbor, discovered since Dickinson first wrote his book.
5. This is the latest estimate for the diameter of the universe. It is possible for the universe to only be 13.7 billion years old, yet 156 billion light years across thanks to the rate of expansion and factors related to the theory of relativity which, quite honestly, I don't understand! See www.space.com/scienceastronomy/mystery_monday_040524.htmlandwww.news.bbc.co.uk/2/hi/science/nature/3753115.stm.

Three
"If You Can't Say Anything Nice . . ."

> *The tongue . . . is a fire, a world of evil among the parts of the*
> *body. It corrupts the whole person, sets the whole course of [one's]*
> *life on fire, and is itself set on fire by hell. . . . No [one] can tame*
> *the tongue. It is a restless evil, full of deadly poison. With the*
> *tongue we praise our Lord and Father, and with it we curse*
> *[human beings], who have been made in God's likeness. Out of the*
> *same mouth come praise and cursing. My brothers [and sisters],*
> *this should not be.*
> —James 3:6-10 NIV

When I was growing up, nearly every kid I knew had a mother who taught him or her "If you can't say something nice about someone, don't say anything at all." This bit of popular wisdom is firmly grounded in the Bible where we're frequently reminded that the "tongue . . . is a fire, a world of evil among the parts of the body," and therefore we're to work to tame the tongue, and to avoid gossip, backbiting, slander, and uttering words that tear others down. Unfortunately, the Christian community has often acted as though these words don't apply to presidents' political parties, and others with whom we disagree. If they don't apply to these, to whom do they apply?

Twice in 2006 I received the same e-mail forwarded to huge lists of Christians. The e-mail was written and designed to inflame Christians against the American Civil Liberties Union (ACLU). In it there were photos of Marines praying, and a note that said the ACLU was up in arms about this. It quoted a supposed ACLU spokesperson named Lucius Traveler about the need to end the practice of Marines praying on federal property. It closed asking people to pray for the Marines and then to be sure to keep the chain going by passing the e-mail on. Apparently, millions of people took this quite seriously. I read this e-mail and thought "Something sounds a bit fishy here." So I took a few minutes to research it, going to the ACLU website where I learned that they were aware of this Internet myth. They have never employed anyone named Lucius Traveler, and they do not oppose prayer; prayer is a civil liberty too.

The crux of this story is the fact that somewhere in Internetland there were Christians who created a fictional character and a fictional story with photos of real Marines praying, and they sent this out to create animosity against the ACLU. And then there were millions of Christians who participated in the slander by passing on the e-mail to all of their friends without taking the time to check out the facts to see if it was true.

It's not just conservative Christians who participate in activities like this. Liberals do the same. We are all afflicted with the same human condition. One of the hallmarks of our tendency to sin is that we feel the need to criticize, we take pleasure in gossiping, and we feel qualified to make judgments, often with very little information.

We slander others for a host of reasons. Perhaps we're jealous of another's success. Maybe we're just insecure. But we also find a tendency to speak ill of others when they disagree with our way of seeing the world. Rather than trying to fully understand why they believe what they believe, and being open to the possibility that we are wrong, we feel threatened by their convictions and look for ways to criticize the individual and his or her convictions. Because talking with those who disagree with us face-to-face about why we think they are wrong might be a bit too threatening, and would require that we listen to their views and arguments, we find it easier to criticize them where it is safe, among friends or like-minded people, on our blogs, or via e-mail.

We say things to our friends *about* these persons we would never say to them face-to-face. We judge their motives and their deeds. Most of us have committed this sin. We have all wounded others by our words. We have misrepresented them, spoken out of turn, and judged them without really taking the time to understand them. Liberals do it, and conservatives do it.

The New Testament speaks to this issue frequently, in part because people struggled with gossip, slander, and criticism as much in the first century as we do today. Jesus tells us in Matthew 5:22c, "If you say, 'You fool,' you will be liable to the hell of fire" and, later in the same sermon, "Do not judge, or you too will be judged. For in the same way you judge others, you will be judged, and with the measure you use, it will be measured to you. Why do you look at the speck of sawdust in your [neighbor's] eye and pay no attention to the plank in your own eye?" (Matthew 7:1-3 NIV). What powerful words they are, and yet how often neglected.

The Apostle Paul says it this way, "Do not let any unwholesome talk come out of your mouths, but only what is helpful for building others up" (Ephesians 4:29 NIV). The Greek word for "unwholesome" is *sapros*. It means rotten, putrid, or worthless—and in this context I believe Paul means to describe, in part, the words we use to destroy others, for in the rest of the verse he contrasts this first form of speech with that which is "helpful for building others up."

> "Do not let any unwholesome talk come out of your mouths, but only what is helpful for building others up."

James is perhaps best known for his words about how we speak about others. He writes, "The tongue . . . is a fire, a world of evil among the parts of the body. It corrupts the whole person, sets the whole course of [one's] life on fire, and is itself set on fire by hell. . . . No [one] can tame the tongue. It is a restless evil, full of deadly poison. With the tongue we praise our Lord and Father, and with it we curse [human beings], who have been made in God's like-ness. Out of the same mouth come praise and cursing. My broth-ers [and sisters], this should not be" (James 3:6, 8-10 NIV).

I would ask again, Does the Lord give us an exemption from practicing the Scriptures when it comes to our political leaders, those who hold office, and others with whom we disagree? Are we al-lowed to lay aside the Golden Rule? Do James's and Paul's and Jesus' words regarding our speech and our enemies no longer apply when discussing those whom we disagree with politically? As James says, "This should not be so!"

> Does the Lord give us an exemption from practicing the Scriptures when it comes to our political leaders, those who hold office, and others with whom we disagree?

This does not mean that we are not to practice discernment. Nor does it mean that we should remain silent in the face of wrongdoing. Yet we can make known our disagreements with oth-ers while doing so in love and with respect for the other. In situa-tions where we must confront individuals, Jesus' guidance in Matthew 18 for how we address wrongs committed against us might be instructive. He tells us to speak to the individual per-sonally, if possible, to discuss the matter in private. If this doesn't resolve the issue, we are to take one or two others with us to be a part of the conversation. And if this still doesn't work, and if the matter is serious enough, we are to bring the matter before our church. If the individual refuses to respond to the church, we are to treat him or her as we would a pagan or tax collector (Matthew 18:15-17). Since Jesus loved tax collectors and sought to minister to them, we can assume that even treating the person as a "tax collector" would require demonstrating love toward him or her.

Part of the polarization we are experiencing in our country today is a result of pastors and church leaders who have abandoned the teachings of Jesus and the apostles regarding the way we speak of those with whom we disagree. Part of the healing of our nation

> Part of the polarization we are experiencing in our country today is a result of pastors and church leaders who have abandoned the teachings of Jesus and the apostles regarding the way we speak of those with whom we disagree.

must come from the church modeling for our society how we are to love those with whom we disagree. Right now we're modeling for society how we destroy with our words and actions those we disagree with.

How can we actually avoid speaking ill of others? Here's what I do when I am at my best and exercising restraint: First, I remember the call of Christ to avoid judging and to avoid calling names (Matthew 5:21-22). My aim is to do Christ's will. Speaking ill of others does not accomplish that aim. Second, I try to search my own heart to see what is behind my need to speak ill of the person. Usually the motivation will be fear, jealousy, insecurity, or revenge. I remind myself of the words of Mark Twain, "Among human beings jealousy ranks distinctly as a weakness; a trademark of small minds." [1] Third, I make it a point to look for the good in the other and to focus on lifting that up rather than pointing out the person's weaknesses. Fourth, I remember the biblical call to humility, and remind myself that I may not be seeing the other person the way God sees him or her. I may not know all the facts. And I remember the many ways in which I fall short of God's plans. By the time I've walked through this mental exercise I find it easier to practice what my mother taught me growing up: If you can't find anything good to say about someone, don't say anything at all.

In many ways the evidence of our faith is found in our ability to control our tongue (or our keyboard). When you find Christians who speak ill of others, who tell half-truths, who resort to name-calling,

> In many ways the evidence of our faith is found in our ability to control our tongue (or our keyboard).

remember the words of Jesus and the apostles and ask if this person reflects the life Christ calls us to. The most important time to ask that question is the next time *you* prepare to hit the "enter" key when you are saying of another "You fool!" or let loose with your own "unwholesome talk."

I've failed to live out the words of this chapter on too many occasions, but they still reflect my aim and ideal.

Looking for the good in those with whom you disagree, expressing enough humility to admit that you may be wrong, and seeking to remove the log from your own eye before removing the splinter from your neighbor's eye—these are characteristics of Christ's followers. And it is in remembering and practicing these Scriptures that Christians will stop being the wedge that divides our nation, and start acting instead as bridge builders and peacemakers that bring an end to the culture wars.

Note

1. Mark Twain, *Letters from the Earth: Uncensored Writings*, ed. Bernard Devoto (New York: Perennial Classics, 2004).

Four
Stage Five: Spiritual Maturity and Gray

Within the true church there is a mysterious unity that over-rides all divisive factors. In groups which in my ignorant piousness I formerly "frowned upon," I have found men so dedicated to Christ and so in love with the truth that I have felt unworthy to be in their presence.
—Billy Graham

I am not the same person I was when I was fourteen. That may be an obvious statement, but it bears mentioning. Neither are you the same person you were when you were fourteen (unless, of course, you are currently fourteen years old). At the time of writing this book I am forty-three. What has changed since I was fourteen? I am twenty pounds heavier. I now have to hold my Bible and any other book at a distance to be able to make out the words. As a result of all the rock concerts I attended at fourteen, I now have to cup my hand around my ear in a restaurant in order to hear and understand what my wife and children are saying to me (a practice that is utterly humiliating to them). But these are not the kind of changes I am thinking about.

I know more today than I did when I was fourteen. Since then I have completed college and graduate school. I have read count-less books, and spent thousands of hours reflecting upon the world, the human condition, and the Bible in order to help me in writing both sermons and books. I have been married for twenty-five years. Living day in and day out with another person has changed me. I have two daughters whose lives and life stages have taught me more about God than I learned in seminary, and whom I love deeply. My wife and daughters have left an indelible mark on my soul.

Much of the change that has happened in my life has been brought about by pastoring and shepherding a congregation of thousands of people over the last seventeen years. I have held the hands of dying people and listened to their words; I have buried too many of their children; I have watched them self-destruct through alcohol or drug abuse, sexual addiction, bitterness, and more. I have seen the worst of humanity in them, but most often, I've seen in them the best of what it means to be human. And serving as their pastor has changed me.

I have had the joy of traveling around the world. I have been with people whose homes have dirt floors and people who have no homes; I have listened to the stories of people who were once our enemies in the former Soviet Union; and I have spent time with people of different religions, and different denominations within the Christian religion, listening to their stories of faith.

Finally, in and through all of this, I believe God has sought to change me, shape me, and make me into what he desires; he is the Potter, and I am the clay. I have often failed in allowing his hand to shape me, but at times, I have felt him breaking me, and remaking me, and most often simply reminding me that he is still by my side, not finished with me yet. And all of this has given me a very different perspective on the world than I had at the age of fourteen. Wouldn't it be odd, and disappointing, if,

Wouldn't it be odd, and disappointing, if, after all of these experiences, I had not grown, changed, or gained a different perspective on life? And yet this is precisely what happens with some people—their faith is unfazed by all of their life experiences. They live unreflective lives and their faith and theological ideas remain exactly as they were when they were fourteen, or perhaps even four.

after all of these experiences, I had not grown, changed, or gained a different perspective on life?

And yet this is precisely what happens with some people— their faith is unfazed by all of their life experiences. They live unreflective lives and their faith and theological ideas remain exactly as they were when they were fourteen, or perhaps even four.

There are others whose life experiences shatter their faith. When their childhood faith is not pliable enough to be stretched with their life experiences, they shed it like a cicada emerging from the ground sheds its brittle exoskeleton before taking flight. They lose their faith as a result of their life experiences and the questions they have asked and reflections they have made concerning God.

The ideal is that your faith not be rigid and unpliable, but instead that it is capable of being stretched and remolded over time, and that your theological and spiritual life grows deeper and more mature with the passing years.

In 1981, Dr. James Fowler of Emory University wrote a book entitled *Stages of Faith*,[1] in which he suggested that there are six stages that religious people may experience in their spiritual and psychological development. Whether Fowler or anyone else can clearly identify all of the stages in faith development, I am uncertain. For many years I dismissed Fowler's work as presumptuous and biased by his own theological perspectives on what constitutes the development of faith. But over time I have come to appreciate the general thesis of his work, and find that it can be helpful as a way of thinking about the changes that can occur in our faith over time.

There's not space in this chapter to offer a comprehensive introduction to Fowler's work; the best introduction is the book itself. Instead I'll offer just a thumbnail sketch of each of the stages as I understand them.

Stage I: Intuitive Projective Faith. This faith is characteristic of children between the ages of three and seven. In this stage children's faith is shaped by their parents and their own imagination and tends toward something akin to a fairy tale. It is difficult for them to differentiate between God and the tooth fairy at this stage.

Stage II: Mythical Literal Faith. This faith is characteristic of school-age children, though some people never emerge from this stage. In Stage II the elements of faith, as it is passed on to the child, are all taken literally. Belief is derived from an external authority and the child can only see these beliefs in the most literal of terms. This faith tends toward simple rules: "If I am good, God will bless me."

Stage III: Synthetic Conventional Faith. Most make the shift to this phase in the teen years. This stage is characterized by conformity with the expectations and beliefs of particular groups or authority figures with little critical examination of the beliefs. One believes a certain way because this is what everyone in his or her particular group or church believes. Many people never leave stage III, but live with an unexamined faith accepted because of the beliefs of others.

Stage IV: Individuative Reflective Faith. This faith is one that has come through trial. Fowler indicates that those who enter this stage do so in their late teens or early twenties, though many don't reach this place until their thirties or forties, and some never do. Here faith is hard and sometimes shattered because, perhaps for the first time, the individual is considering questions and challenges to his or her faith. Individuals are claiming their faith for themselves and not simply the faith that belonged to a parent or authority figure. The individual will demythologize in this stage, beginning to recognize that some beliefs were more symbolic than literal, and differentiating between them.

Most people remain in stage III, with not a few, I think, remaining in stage II, for most of their lives. Both of these stages lend themselves to black and white, absolutes, and certainties. Stage IV will represent a faith crisis and struggle, dark nights of the soul, and times of intense doubt.

Stage V: Conjunctive Faith. This stage, in which the word *conjunctive* means to "join things together," often occurs around age forty, as the individual passes through the trials of stage IV and comes to accept paradox, the situation in which seemingly contradictory things are at one and the same time true, in which seemingly irreconcilable ideas can be held together, and in which seemingly absurd things are actually real. In this stage people become more open to and tolerant of the views of others. They come to appreciate that the world is more gray than black and white.

> In this stage people become more open to and tolerant of the views of others. They come to appreciate that the world is more gray than black and white.

Stage VI: Universalizing Faith. Fowler says that this stage of faith characterized by selflessness, unconditional love, and a willingness to suffer on behalf of others is extremely rare. Fowler's picture of these persons would be a Mother Teresa or a Martin Luther King, Jr. John Wesley spoke of this as Christian perfection or sanctification.

Fowler's stages have something to say to Christians. One may never move beyond stage III, and yet still seek to be yielded to Christ, experience God in profound ways, and live selflessly. Likewise, the move from stage III to stage V is not easy. It often only comes as a result of hardship, tragedy, or struggle that shatters our simplistic understanding of God and faith and the world around us and leaves us with a faith that is deeper, more humble, and more open to mystery and paradox.

One of my parishioners who studied Fowler's work came to me after a particular sermon that challenged the black-and-white thinking of some in my congregation and said, "Adam, the problem is that most people in the world will never leave stages II or III and you are challenging this congregation to enter stage V. They'll never be able to do it." I appreciated this man's assessment of why the particular sermon I preached was so unsettling to some, yet I cannot accept the fact that people cannot move beyond stage III.

Our culture is in the midst of an important shift in which more people will be able to accept paradox and to hold fast to a compelling faith while living with ambiguity.

I have two pictures of stage V faith: my aunt Celia Bell and Billy Graham. Both came from very conservative church backgrounds (Celia Bell from the Church of Christ and Billy Graham from the Southern Baptist denomination). Both hold fast to particular doctrines and views of the Christian gospel. Yet both my aunt and Billy Graham experienced times of challenge and tragedy that led them to question their early assumptions about life and faith. Both came to the place where they held to their convictions while recognizing that others, with whom they disagreed, could be their brothers and sisters in Christ. They came to embrace paradox and ambiguity even as they held to their strong convictions. Graham came to mandate that his crusades be integrated events even as many in the South believed that the "separation of the races" was a biblical idea. He also came to embrace and work with Roman Catholics and mainline Protestants, and for both of these decisions he received ample criticism from those in his own movement who felt he was "compromising the gospel."

My Aunt Celia Bell made a similar journey. She is a part of the Church of Christ—a conservative church that holds such literal interpretations of the Scriptures that they refuse to allow the use of musical instruments in worship because the New Testament does not mention any of these instruments being used in a worship setting. (One benefit of this, however, is that Church of Christ folks know how to *sing*; their a cappella singing is beautiful!) She loves her church and has been a lifelong member. But when I speak to her now, at age ninety-two, I find that her faith is much broader than that held by some in her denomination. As a result of her love of learning, she sees a broad array of denominations as being authentically Christian, and she thinks that often we make "mountains out of molehills" when it comes to our human opinions. What I love most about her is how she's able to see good and truth in those who hold very different opinions from her own.

I appreciated these words of Billy Graham, captured in an article in the *Christian Century*:

> I am now aware that the family of God contains people of various ethnological, cultural, class, and denominational differences. . . . Within the true church there is a mysterious unity that overrides all divisive factors. In groups which in my ignorant piousness I formerly "frowned upon," I have found men so dedicated to Christ and so in love with the truth that I have felt unworthy to be in their presence. I have learned that although Christians do not always agree, they can disagree agreeably, and that what is most needed today is for us to show an unbelieving world that we love one another.[2]

The August 14, 2006, *Newsweek* cover story on Billy Graham highlighted the changes that have happened in the evangelist's thinking and spirit over the years. His daughter, Anne Graham Lotz, in commenting on her brother Franklin Graham's more conservative stance on certain issues and how it contrasts with their father's views, said, "When Daddy was my brother's age, he was saying some pretty strong things, too, so you have to remember that experience and the living of a life can soften your perspective."[3] In the article Dr. Graham was asked to describe how his faith had changed over the years. Jon Meacham, the author of the story, wrote,

> He is an evangelist still unequivocally committed to the Gospel, but increasingly thinks God's ways and means are veiled from human eyes and wrapped in mystery. "There are many things

that I don't understand," he says. He does not believe that Christians need to take every verse of the Bible literally; "sincere Christians," he says, "can disagree about the details of Scripture and theology. . . . I'm not a literalist in the sense that every single jot and tittle is from the Lord," Graham says. "This is a little difference in my thinking through the years."[4]

That little change is actually quite momentous. The article was magnificent in demonstrating the deep faith of Billy Graham *and* in showing how that faith has changed over the years.

I served as one of the leaders of the last Billy Graham Crusade in Kansas City and in that capacity had the opportunity to meet with Billy Graham on three occasions. My experience of him was quite moving. Here was a man who is probably the best-known living Christian, who preaches a very simple, evangelical gospel, yet who was gracious, broad-minded, and reflected a humility born of years of experience. These facts have led him to a stage V kind of faith that recognizes that life is more complex, on the one hand, than he had earlier in his life supposed, and at the same time, recognizes that life may be simpler than he once believed.

I would add one postscript here about maturing in faith. I was speaking about Fowler's stages with one of the associate pastors at my church. She noted that for many people who have been brought up on ambiguity and raised in the religious left, maturing in the faith may include learning to embrace certainties and gaining a greater comfort with doctrinal formulations and convictions. My faith journey began on the right, with a much more concrete, literal, and black-and-white faith shaped in the conservative tradition. Maturing in faith has, I believe, led me to the center. Perhaps when people start on the left, with a faith that is already very ambiguous, their journeys lead them to the center as well. For them that means an embrace of more structure, certainty, and doctrinal convic-

> Perhaps when people start on the left, with a faith that is already very ambiguous, their journeys lead them to the center as well.

tion, just as it meant a shedding of some certainty and an openness to ambiguity for me. In the end, perhaps, both those on the left and those on the right are meant to meet in the middle.

Jesus taught us to have faith like that of a child. By this I believe he meant the wide-eyed wonder and simple trust that children have in God. I don't believe he meant that we were to avoid cultivating a faith that is thoughtful, reflective, and able to recognize and embrace paradox and ambiguity. Stages IV and V are the stages where we finally accept that the world is not always black and white and when we come to appreciate the reality of gray.

Notes

1. James Fowler, *Stages of Faith* (New York: Harper & Row, 1981).
2. As cited by Harold Myra and Marshall Shelley in "Leading with Love" at www.christianitytoday.com/tc/2005/005/2.40.html.
3. Jon Meacham, "A Pilgrim's Progress," *Newsweek* (August 14, 2006), http://www.newsweek.com/id/46365.
4. Ibid.

Five
Finding the Sweet Spot

Most types of sports equipment like a golf club, a tennis rac-
quet or a baseball bat have a certain spot that, if the ball hits it, will
give the player the optimal result. Hitting this sweet spot yields a
long drive down the fairway, a swift crosscourt return or home run
swing. Every sport has a sweet spot of some type. If you have expe-
rienced it, you know when you hit the sweet spot, you barely feel
it. The ball goes where you want it to go—even further and faster.
Doesn't get any better than that!
—Lee Colan[1]

While I was a student at Oral Roberts University (ORU) there
was an extensive code of dress and behavior. No alcohol,
no sex (unless you were married), no swearing, no facial hair, no
skipping chapel. At registration, the length of men's hair was
checked and they were sent to the back of the line for a haircut if
their hair touched the collars of their shirts. Ties for men and skirts
for women were required dress. At one point faculty could not be
divorced (though this changed after Oral's son, Richard, was divorced). All of this tied to a certain concept of what holiness
might look like.

I graduated from college and went to seminary at Southern
Methodist University (SMU). Blue jeans and T-shirts were fine,
chapel was not required, and facial hair and long hair for men were
allowed. Even a few of the seminary faculty swore. Though not
talked about openly it was assumed that singles might be having
sex. One of my first surprises came when a female student told me
during the first week of seminary that she always did her best evangelism over a six-pack of beer! These might represent a picture of

the two poles of legalism and libertinism that have existed within Christianity from its earliest days. Neither ORU nor SMU represented the extremes of these poles, but while ORU had leaned toward legalism, SMU leaned toward libertinism. More broadly speaking, conservatives have a natural tendency toward legalism and liberals toward libertinism.

I'm a lousy golfer. When I swing the club my ball generally either hooks to the left and ends up in the creek, or it slices to the right and ends up in the woods. But the ideal is to hit the ball in such a way that it lands on the short grasses of the fairway. There is a place on the club face where the ideal amount of energy is transferred from the club to the ball. That place is called the "sweet spot," and you can always tell when you've hit the ball from the sweet spot by the wonderful sound it makes. I've never personally heard that sound come from my clubs, but I've heard it from other golfers! And when you hit the ball from that spot, it tends to travel long and straight.

Christianity, when most effective, most faithful, and most empowering, is found in the sweet spot between legalism and libertinism. It holds together, in tension, the seemingly opposite ideas of grace and holiness, faith and works, legalism and libertinism.

Black and white are found at the poles: The legalists are ready to judge all who don't live the gospel according to their rules, and their rules have served to push many away from Christ. The libertines have often failed to recognize that there are boundaries, that there could be anything we should refrain from doing simply because the act itself might displease God. The Christian life is found in the sweet spot between these two.

> Christianity, when most effective, most faithful, and most empowering, is found in the sweet spot between legalism and libertinism. It holds together, in tension, the seemingly opposite ideas of grace and holiness, faith and works, legalism and libertinism.

In the sixth century before Christ, the prophet Jeremiah had foretold that the days would come when God would make a new covenant with his people, different from the covenant he had made with them in Sinai through Moses. In that covenant God gave them the Law and demanded obedience to it in exchange for his protection and care for Israel. Most of the Old Testament is the story of Israel's failure to live up to this covenant. As a result, God spoke through Jeremiah. He said:

> The days are surely coming, says the LORD, when I will make a new covenant with the house of Israel and the house of Judah. It will not be like the covenant that I made with their ancestors when I took them by the hand to bring them out of the land of Egypt—a covenant that they broke, though I was their husband, says the LORD. But this is the covenant that I will make with the house of Israel after those days, says the LORD: I will put my law within them, and I will write it on their hearts; and I will be their God, and they shall be my people. No longer shall they teach one another, or say to each other, "Know the LORD," for they shall all know me, from the least of them to the greatest, says the LORD; for I will forgive their iniquity, and remember their sin no more. (Jeremiah 31:31-34)

Christians find this passage from the Hebrew Bible especially illuminating. At the Last Supper Jesus, anticipating his death, took a cup of wine and said to them, "This cup is the new covenant in my blood. Do this, as often as you drink it, in remembrance of me" (1 Corinthians 11:25). So Christians understood that what God had promised through Jeremiah God was fulfilling in Jesus Christ. He was entering into a new covenant or binding relationship with humanity. No longer would humanity be expected to strive to fulfill the Law of Moses, with its demands for circumcision, ritual acts of holiness, and a whole host of laws. Instead God would write his law, his desire for his people, on their hearts, and all people would know him and he would forgive their sins.

This was a radical and revolutionary idea in the early church. It was liberating—and terrifying. Some early Christians rejected this idea, believing that while Jesus offered forgiveness and put a face to God, Christians were still to follow the law. In the law was safety, and black-and-white requirements, boundaries, and structure. They continued to insist that Christians be circumcised and become Jews in order to follow Jesus.

But the Apostle Paul rejected this interpretation of the new covenant. He had lived under the law his whole life. And he saw that through Jesus the old covenant had been fulfilled, the contract God had with humanity was marked "paid in full," and now God had entered into a new covenant with humankind through Jesus Christ. This new covenant was indeed radical. God had, in advance, made provision for the sins of the world. He had demonstrated his love, grace, and mercy, and had offered eternal life. All we had to do was accept this gift of salvation—to trust in Jesus Christ and to accept God's offer of salvation.

But how do we live in response to this great gift of salvation? This was the question that had to be answered. Paul noted that God had placed his Spirit in the hearts of all who believe. Christ's followers seek to follow the example of Christ as we listen for the leadership of the Spirit. We desire to honor and please God and to do the right thing. But now, rather than following a set of laws dictating to us what the right thing is, we must be led by the Spirit; and with the joy of the already forgiven, rather than the fear of those hoping to be forgiven, we seek to please the Lord.

Some misinterpreted Paul's approach to the gospel, believing that they could do anything they wanted, live any way they wanted, with absolute freedom, provided they had faith in Christ. James, in the New Testament, offers a corrective to this thinking when he says, "faith without works is dead" (James 2:20 KJV).

Paul stood firmly against these persons, sometimes called libertines or antinomians, who seemed, to him, to advocate an "anything goes" approach to life. In Romans 6:15 he writes, "What then? Should we sin because we are not under law but under grace? By no means!" In Philippians 3:18-19 he speaks of the libertines in the most unflattering of ways: "For many live as enemies of the cross of Christ; I have often told you of them, and now I tell you even with tears. Their end is destruction; their god is the belly;

"I therefore, the prisoner in the Lord, beg you to lead a life worthy of the calling to which you have been called" (Ephesians 4:1).

and their glory is in their shame; their minds are set on earthly things." Consequently, he makes statements like these: "I therefore, the prisoner in the Lord, beg you to lead a life worthy of the calling to which you have been called" (Ephesians 4:1), and "I appeal to you therefore, brothers and sisters, by the mercies of God, to present your bodies as a living sacrifice, holy and acceptable to God, which is your spiritual worship. Do not be conformed to this world, but be transformed by the renewing of your minds, so that you may discern what is the will of God—what is good and acceptable and perfect" (Romans 12:1-2).

Yet while calling the believers to holiness, Paul rejects the idea of legalism. Paul writes his epistle to the Galatians in great frustration and anguish. Legalistic Christians had come to Galatia after Paul had founded the church there. They began to teach that these new Christian converts needed to be circumcised and to attempt to live according to the Law of Moses. Listen to Paul's response to these legalists:

> I am astonished that you are so quickly deserting the one who called you in the grace of Christ and are turning to a different gospel. (1:6)

> We know that a person is justified not by the works of the law but through faith in Jesus Christ. And we have come to believe in Christ Jesus, so that we might be justified by faith in Christ, and not by doing the works of the law, because no one will be justified by the works of the law. (2:16)

> If justification comes through the law, then Christ died for nothing. You foolish Galatians! Who has bewitched you? . . . The only thing I want to learn from you is this: Did you receive the Spirit by doing the works of the law or by believing what you heard? (2:21b–3:2)

For freedom Christ has set us free. Stand firm, therefore, and do not submit again to a yoke of slavery. (5:1)

There is such passion in Paul's letter to the Galatians because he sees the very essence of the gospel at stake. Christ came so that we might have freedom and not be slaves to the law any longer. Yet even in Galatians Paul seeks to navigate between legalism and libertinism. He writes to those who might be tempted to think "anything goes" now that they've been justified by faith:

When we can hold together, in tension, the call to freedom that comes by grace and the call to holiness in seeking to live by the Spirit, we find the sweet spot—the perfect balance between grace and holiness—that allows our faith to soar.

You were called to freedom, brothers and sisters; only do not use your freedom as an opportunity for self-indulgence, but through love become slaves to one another. For the whole law is summed up in a single commandment, "You shall love your neighbor as yourself." If, however, you bite and devour one another, take care that you are not consumed by one another.

Live by the Spirit, I say, and do not gratify the desires of the flesh. For what the flesh desires is opposed to the Spirit, and what the Spirit desires is opposed to the flesh; for these are opposed to each other, to prevent you from doing what you want. But if you are led by the Spirit, you are not subject to the law. (Galatians 5:13-18)

Paul says similar things in all of his letters. He comes dangerously close, at times, to setting up a new law as he tries to illustrate what the works of the flesh look like in his day and time, but he always comes short of it, challenging the believers to live by the

Spirit, to allow the Spirit to guide them, and to seek to use their freedom. Note how Paul here has said the entire law and prophets could be summed up in one commandment: "Love your neighbor as yourself." James cites this same passage as well, calling it the "royal law." Both Paul and James draw from Jesus, who repeatedly notes that this is the second great commandment after the call to love God. He, too, notes that it summarizes all the law and the prophets.

Finding the sweet spot between legalism and libertinism is not easy. We continue to struggle with it to this very day. Liberalism is the pull toward personal freedom that can easily result in libertinism. Conservativism tends to draw toward rules, laws, and a legalism that so easily negates the power of the gospel. But when we can hold together, in tension, the call to freedom that comes by grace and the call to holiness in seeking to live by the Spirit, we find the sweet spot—the perfect balance between grace and holiness—that allows our faith to soar.

Note

1. Lee Colan, "Optimize Your Sweet Spot," www.articlear.com/Article/Optimize-Your-Sweet-Spot/21601.

Six
Shhh! Just Listen!

You must understand this, my beloved: let everyone be quick to listen, slow to speak.
—James 1:19

One of the struggles I face is simply to listen. Pastors tend to be people with strong convictions. I've had to train myself, over the years, to listen to others more and to talk less, and, even so, I still fail at this many times. You've no doubt heard it said that God gave us two ears and only one mouth in direct proportion to how much he intends us to use them. The Letter of James offers us wonderful guidance: "Let everyone be quick to listen, slow to speak, slow to anger" (James 1:19b).

One of the reasons for today's culture wars is the unwillingness of people on either the left or the right to listen to those with whom they disagree. They are quick to speak, and quick to anger, but slow to listen.

Early in my ministry I was visiting with a man whose theology had been shaped by the New Age books he had read. He was a terrific guy, but his beliefs were quite unorthodox. He had been visiting our church and found it interesting, but he recognized that we did not see eye-to-eye on some things. As I listened to him I had a

43

tremendous urge to correct his theology, to help him "see the light." I am grateful I did not act on this impulse. Instead I just listened and occasionally offered words like "That's an interesting perspective. While it's not what I've believed, I'll give that some thought." If he asked, "What do you believe?" I'd share with him my perspective, but with gentleness and humility. If he didn't ask, I didn't share it.

Years later, this man became a tremendous leader in the church. Over time he sorted through the theological issues. He came to understand more clearly the claims of the Christian faith and embraced them. And he has mentored many others in their faith. But had I acted upon my need to correct him, debate him, and set him straight in our first encounter, I don't think he would have come to this place in his faith. The key to his growth in faith was allowing him to consider alternatives while gently offering additional perspectives for him to think about, *and* to simply listen without immediately trying to correct.

This lesson is one I have to constantly remember. When my wife speaks to me about something she's struggling with, she's not looking for me to solve the problem for her; she just wants someone with whom to talk it through. She wants to know I'm actually listening, that I care, and yes, for me to offer an *occasional* bit of feedback. But the value of the conversation isn't in my thinking of a solution to her dilemma; it is in allowing her to talk about it aloud.

In pastoral counseling the same is true. Yes, I will offer suggestions and Scriptures that might point to principles that give hope or guidance. But listening and showing concern are the most important gift I offer.

I've also found that listening is not only important for the other person, it's important for me. I once spent seven weeks studying Christian denominations other than my own, interviewing pastors and denominational leaders, and attending worship in these traditions. While all seven shared the beliefs summarized by the Apostles' and Nicene creeds, they differed markedly in certain aspects of faith and practice. I often went into the interviews thinking I knew more about the particular denomination than I really did. But as I listened to each of the clergy from the various

traditions, allowed myself to experience the unique worship expressions, and then studied their history and doctrines, I found my
own faith and life were enriched, and I gained a deep appreciation for each of the denominations and traditions.

I went on to share these insights with our congregation. I
preached an eight-week series of sermons retracing church history,
theology, and Christian spirituality by looking at the different denominations I had studied. Our worship team studied the worship
practices of the different denominations and we actually designed
worship each week so that our parishioners could experience what
worship is like in the other traditions. On Orthodox Sunday we included icons, incense, and the Orthodox liturgy. We experienced
a Catholic mass the following week. On the weekend we studied
Pentecostalism, we invited people to raise their hands in worship
and to pray aloud together extemporaneously, inviting the Holy
Spirit to fill them. And each week, rather than trying to pick apart
and criticize the other denominations, we sought to understand, to
appreciate, and to learn from our brothers and sisters in these other
churches. The only way we could do that was by listening to them.
Our entire congregation was enriched by the experience and I
eventually wrote a book summarizing what I had learned. [1]

At the time several people asked me, "Aren't you worried that
people might leave your church to go to one of the others if you
preach this series?" I think in order to listen and learn from others, and to lead others in a study like this, you have to both feel
some level of confidence and security in what you believe and be
willing to risk that someone will find one of the other churches
more appealing, or discover that these churches possess a bit more
of the truth than does one's own tradition. I mentioned this question to our congregation and told them, "If one of you discovered
in this series that you would be better able to grow and to serve
God in another tradition, I would consider that a success. Now,
I'm hoping that's not going to happen to half our congregation!
I'm guessing most of you landed here because this church ministers to you and connects with you. But we're not afraid to study,
learn from, and listen to other denominations." I don't know of

anyone who left our church, but there were thousands who came away with a deeper faith and an ability to appreciate their friends of other traditions. It was awesome.

That leads me to one last thought. The culture wars we're experiencing now, and the polarization in our society and in the church, are, in large part, a result of our unwillingness to listen to others and acknowledge that they may have something important to say. Consequently, we talk past one another, but seldom really attempt to learn from one another, or to see if there is any place where, despite our differences, we might come to find common ground.

In a country polarized between the left and the right, and a world that is plagued by terrorism, violence, and war, hope is not found in people on both sides shouting their views louder, but in people learning to listen, and actually hear, what others are saying.

The book of Proverbs offers this wisdom: "Fools think their own way is right, / but the wise listen to advice" (12:15).

The wise don't simply listen to advice, however. They listen to people as they share their perspectives, insights, and understandings.

In a country polarized between the left and the right, and a world that is plagued by terrorism, violence, and war, hope is not found in people on both sides shouting their views louder, but in people learning to listen, and actually hear, what others are saying.

Seeing gray in a world of black and white requires a willingness to risk, a self-confidence that allows you to not be driven by fear, and most important, a willingness to listen.

Note

1. See Adam Hamilton, *Christianity's Family Tree: What Other Christians Believe and Why* (Nashville: Abingdon Press, 2007). This is both a book and a small-group study with videos and a leader's guide.

S e v e n
Being Pentecostal without Losing Your Mind

> You will receive power when the Holy Spirit has come upon you.
> —Acts 1:8

> For if I pray in a tongue, my spirit prays but my mind is unproductive. What should I do then? I will pray with the spirit, but I will pray with the mind also; I will sing praise with the spirit, but I will sing praise with the mind also. Otherwise, if you say a blessing with the spirit, how can anyone in the position of an outsider say the "Amen" to your thanksgiving, since the outsider does not know what you are saying? For you may give thanks well enough, but the other person is not built up. I thank God that I speak in tongues more than all of you; nevertheless, in church I would rather speak five words with my mind, in order to instruct others also, than ten thousand words in a tongue.
> —1 Corinthians 14:14-19

In the twentieth century, Pentecostalism and its sibling charismatic traditions swept over the United States and the world. The use of the wildfire metaphor is not inappropriate. Imagine a massive forest suffering from drought. The groundcover and the trees are so dry that the slightest spark can start a fire that soon spreads to tens of thousands of acres, igniting everything in its path. This was the situation in the twentieth-century church.

The church spoke primarily to the cognitive side of the individual. It offered guidance, moral teaching, theology, and a call to service. It provided community and identity. But many churches had lost the capacity to help people experience the presence of God, or to help them feel at all. Worship, even in nonliturgical churches, was predictable. People were spiritually dry and longing to experience something that would touch their souls.

Frances may have typified this. She was one of the great saints of the church I served just out of seminary. She would do anything for her Lord or her church. As a part of our evangelistic outreach, Francis, in her late seventies, helped me, each week, divide and then deliver our altar flowers in small bouquets to the first-time visitors at the church where I was an associate pastor.

One week Frances had surgery. When I went to see her in the convalescent center, we began to talk about our faith. She told me, with tears in her eyes, that in all her life as a Christian she had never once actually felt God's presence. Frances was like one of those trees in the forest, dry from drought and longing for an experience with God.

In the early 1900s when the Pentecostal movement took off, it offered people a wild, untamable, emotional experience that was attributed to the outpouring of the Holy Spirit. The movement spread most quickly, at first, among those who were less inclined to skepticism and analyzing such things, but who were simply ready to receive the experience that the Pentecostal churches named the baptism of the Holy Spirit. By the 1950s the fire leaped from the Pentecostal churches into the mainline churches through

the charismatic renewal movement, creating strife and divisions along the way between
those who were skeptical or
even threatened by this movement and those who had taken
the plunge. Sometimes those

Sometimes those persons newly
"baptized in the Holy Spirit" didn't
know how to handle the experience.

persons newly "baptized in the Holy Spirit" didn't know how to
handle the experience. They began to struggle with the same affliction suffered at Corinth where the believers became prideful in
their spiritual gifts.

It was 1978 when I was invited, at fourteen, to attend a small
Pentecostal church in our community. At the time I did not believe in God, but I did believe in girls, and I met three cute girls
there the first weekend I attended this church. My previous church
experience was limited to attending Roman Catholic mass with
my grandmother and a three-year stint in The United Methodist
Church that ended when my parents divorced when I was twelve.
This Pentecostal church was quite different from either of the two
churches I had previously attended. There was an emotionalism or
passion that I was not used to, or comfortable with at first. There
were odd things that would happen in worship—people raising
their hands as they sang, closing their eyes and earnestly worshiping God, praying aloud fervently, and, from time to time, voicing
outbursts of messages in what sounded to me like gibberish, followed by an "interpretation" in English shortly after.

It was in this church, after some six months of worshiping and
reading my Bible, that I came to trust in Christ, surrendering my
life to him and committing to follow him. The pastor told me that
the next stop in my spiritual journey was to be baptized in the Holy
Spirit. I, and the other kids in the youth group, would come to the
front of the church every week pleading with God to give us this
gift. Our pastor told us we would know when we had actually received it, for the evidence was speaking in tongues. Week after
week we would pray. But nothing happened.

For me the experience came one night after I had come home
from church. I was praying next to my bed, and as I did so I could

imagine words or syllables forming in my mind that I began to speak. As I did this, it felt as though my tongue had been freed from the confines of English vocabulary and grammar. It was like praying with the heart, pouring out whatever feelings I was having to God at a purely emotional level. Paul notes, "Likewise the Spirit helps us in our weakness; for we do not know how to pray as we ought, but that very Spirit intercedes with sighs too deep for words" (Romans 8:26). The words I was speaking and the experience I was having at that time were like expressing emotions that were "too deep for words."

In the years since that time I have come to understand the experience of speaking in tongues and the baptism of the Holy Spirit differently than I did at fourteen. I believe that every believer has the gift of the Holy Spirit, and that tongues is not *the* evidence, but perhaps rather *an* evidence, of the outpouring of the Holy Spirit. I don't believe we receive a second outpouring of the Holy Spirit, but instead we continually learn to be more open to the work and power of the Holy Spirit in our lives.

I left the Pentecostal movement in 1983, while in college, yearning for something that would feed my intellect as much as my emotions. I landed in The United Methodist Church, which felt, at the time, to be nearly a polar opposite to the church I had come from. While the Pentecostal church I had attended was filled with passion and emotion, the United Methodist church I attended reflected a quiet reverence and was a bit reserved. The Pentecostal church had sermons preached with fervor, that aroused the soul but which, at times, lacked substance, while The United Methodist Church I attended had sermons of lower decibel levels, but which I would remember and reflect on following worship.

A story that may capture the differences between the two traditions is exemplified by an experience I had at seventeen when I was preparing to graduate from high school and go away to college in order to study for the ministry. A well-educated woman in the Pentecostal church I attended discouraged me from going into the ministry. She said, "Adam, God has given you a keen intellect. You need to use it. Anyone can be a pastor—you don't have to have particularly strong intellectual skills to do the job. You don't even have to go to college to be ordained. But you have this gift—you need to go into a career where you will use it." This woman's perception of the ordained ministry in the Pentecostal movement is not entirely accurate, but it captured what was, for many in Pentecostalism, a belief that education and the cultivation of the intellect were of less importance than passion, particularly for clergy.

Today, in many conservative churches, pastors are not required to have any theological training at all. One can be ordained by another pastor in a worship service even if the candidate has had no training, no education, and the church has conducted no background check.[1] Laity in these churches entrust their theological and spiritual formation to people who may have a gift for speaking, but who know little, if any, more than

Today, in many conservative churches, pastors are not required to have any theological training at all. One can be ordained by another pastor in a worship service even if the candidate has had no training, no education, and the church has conducted no background check.

they do. Sometimes these pastors know nothing of the history of the church or how the Bible was formed, they have not wrestled with the difficult questions of faith, and they have received no formal training in pastoral counseling, biblical interpretation, or theology.

I have a friend, a younger pastor who had very little theological training before he was ordained. He and I meet together every couple of months for breakfast. As much as I would love to see him go back to school, this may not be possible for him. But what I love about him is that he is a voracious reader. He is pursuing extensive study and inviting others to mentor him. His reading and study have added a depth to his preaching and teaching and ministry that is, in turn, helping shape Christians of depth in his congregation.

For centuries the most educated person in a community was the pastor. Most of the historic universities around the world were formed to train clergy. But somehow, in America today, many Christians seem to think that proper training is not important, and that it may even be a detriment to ministry. No one would go to a heart surgeon who had never been to medical school, or a lawyer who hadn't been to law school. But we routinely invite people to shape our souls who may have little more than charisma going for them.

I'm reminded of the conversation two bishops had concerning a pastor they heard preaching. The one said, "He's quite a speaker," to which the other replied, "He's got a lot of merchandise in the showroom, but he's got nothing back in the storeroom."

Again, I am not proposing every pastor needs a master of divinity degree, but every pastor should be well read, should be constantly seeking to learn, and should see the intellect as one of the gifts God has given him or her in order to disciple people.

For decades there was a migration of people from the mainline churches to the Pentecostal and charismatic churches. More recently, the tide has been moving the other direction. Many clergy and laity entering The United Methodist Church today, and presumably other mainline churches, are coming out of the Pentecostal and charismatic traditions, looking for something different. They appreciate the traditions, the concern for justice, and the way in which the church speaks to the intellect.

Here, too, I believe we have two poles: the intellect and the heart. These may also be expressed in terms of reason and experience. Do we really have to choose between pursuing our faith with the intellect—asking critical questions, and bringing our best reasoning to bear on our faith—or enjoying a deeply emotional, passionate, and heartfelt faith that moves us? The truth is, we need a balance of the two. Some of us are more right-brained, and some more left-brained. But we all have both emotive and cognitive dimensions and needs.

Too often the challenge for mainline pastors, and one of the reasons churches began to be cautious about an educated clergy, is allowing our education to diminish our passion. When you focus on the intellect, and you devote yourself to study, there is a tendency to become a bit more broadminded, but often this comes at the expense of conviction and passion. It is important that we not let this happen. We cannot afford to have a "reasonless" Christianity, but neither can we afford a passionless one.

> We cannot afford to have a "reasonless" Christianity, but neither can we afford a passionless one.

John Wesley and those belonging to the early Methodist movement managed to hold these two dimensions together in creative tension. Wesley was at times called a "reasonable enthusiast." To be an enthusiast in eighteenth-century England was to be associated with spiritual passion—what was considered to be in excess by many prim and proper Brits. But Wesley balanced this enthusiasm for God (the very word *enthusiasm* means, literally, to be filled with God) with an ability to speak to the intellect. His preaching was theologically informed, biblical, and reflected the vast amount of reading and study he had done in his life.

His preaching was partnered with the rousing hymnody of his brother Charles—who was writing what amounted to contemporary worship music for his day. The songs were meant to be memorized and then sung "lustily" (but not so loud as to disrupt others).

John Wesley had known personally what it was to experience an assurance of salvation that came from a touch of the Holy Spirit. His best-known report of such an experience occurred in 1738 while attending a meeting of a religious society. He noted that "I felt my heart strangely warmed, and I did trust in Christ, Christ alone for my salvation." This experience of the warmed heart profoundly shaped Wesley in the months following it. Many in the services where Wesley preached had profound experiences of the Spirit. Yet Wesley was always also cautious of emotional excess.

In our Christian life, and in our churches, I believe we must find that place where experience and reason, the heart and the intellect, are held together in a wonderful tension in which each provides an important balance and counterweight to the other. I believe this will be the great hunger of the twenty-first century: a faith that doesn't require suspension of the intellect, but draws upon it, while at the same time remaining a faith in which God's presence is experienced, in which our hearts are "strangely warmed," and in which the power of the Holy Spirit is welcomed and embraced.

Too often in the Pentecostal expressions of the Christian faith, passion without the appropriate balance of reason led to unfortunate

> I believe this will be the great hunger of the twenty-first century: a faith that doesn't require suspension of the intellect but draws upon it, while at the same time remaining a faith in which God's presence is experienced.

excesses, theological expressions that were barely recognizable as Christian, and a spirituality that was primarily built upon emotion. Too often in a host of traditions from the conservative to the mainline churches, we've had just the opposite—a kind of Enlightenment, propositional faith that fed the intellect but left the soul empty, dry, and devoid of the Spirit's power. What we need is preaching, worship, and spiritual disciplines that will help us reclaim a "reasonable enthusiasm."

One final thought about Pentecostalism: One of the great legacies of Pentecostalism will be its reminder to the church of the availability, power, and work of the Holy Spirit. Jesus taught that the Holy Spirit would comfort, guide, lead, convict, and empower his people. It was the Holy Spirit's work on the Day of Pentecost that gave birth to the church and transformed the disciples from frightened followers to bold witnesses

> One of the great legacies of Pentecostalism will be its reminder to the church of the availability, power, and work of the Holy Spirit. Jesus taught that the Holy Spirit would comfort, guide, lead, convict, and empower his people.

willing to risk persecution and death for their faith. Clearly, we need this Pentecostal power in our churches and in our lives. We need to listen for the leading of the Holy Spirit, discover the boldness and courage that comes with the power of the Holy Spirit, and be open to the stirring of the heart that comes with an authentic encounter with the Holy Spirit. Actively seeking the Spirit's work, allowing God to touch our emotions, while pursuing a faith that speaks to the intellect is one more example of a faith that seeks a balance between black and white—a faith that embraces gray.

Note

1. The official website of the Southern Baptist Convention (see www.sbc.net/aboutus/faqs.asp#2), for instance, notes that there is "no standard

process or policy" concerning ordination and that each local church is allowed to ordain anyone they choose, and is free to decide whether their pastors even need to be ordained. Some congregations require seminary training and some do not. This is true for a large number of independent churches as well. Increasingly, even conservative churches are requiring some biblical and theological training.

Part II
The Bible, Beliefs, and the Spiritual Journey

Vida was reading the Bible (her first time through) and she had a look of disgust on her face. Each night she reads, it seems to be a different look of disgust, like she's continually shocked and horrified. Being a Christian for just over a year, these stories we cherish and love were quite a shock to her. I got in bed, looked at her and said, "What is it this time?"

Depending on the night and what stories she was reading, it would be "David had to go get 100 Philistine foreskins for Saul" or "David killed Uriah for his wife" or "Solomon is having a lot of sex with his whorish wives" or "Absalom had sex with his father's women" or "Abimelech killed all 70 of his brothers . . ." Each time, her eyebrows are wrinkled in that certain way that seems to suggest that when she has a chance, she's going to have a little chit-chat with God and what in the world he may have been thinking when he penned this or that little number.

It's in these moments that I feel sorry for God.

—Zachary Forrest y Salazar[1]

Eight
The Battle over the Bible²

It ain't those parts of the Bible that I can't understand that bother me, it is the parts that I do understand.
—Mark Twain

I spent 6 long . . . years in a black and white church and it almost killed me or at least my spirit. I have no verses to quote but I can say I dig the gray area, not because it leaves me room to twist His word, but it gives me room to understand it, make it real. I struggled with the hundreds of contradictions in the bible, until I left the . . . mindwarping church I was stuck in. I got saved again, and tasted grace. God gave us a brain, we should use it and try to wrap it around His word.
—posted on a blog by "Strada"

What is the Bible? Is it simply a collection of ancient writings describing the faith and insights of Israelites and the first followers of Jesus, capturing their biases, their cultural situations, and their prescientific worldviews? Or is it the Word of God with every word having been chosen by God, the human authors merely functioning as secretaries or scribes? Is it marked by the authors' transient and ever-evolving views of God and humanity, and by the unique character of the authors and the needs of the communities to which the books were written? Or is it, on all of its pages, in every one of its verses, timeless truth, transcending culture, and applicable to all cultures at all times? Is it, as a collection of documents written by fallible human beings, capable of erring in its facts and interpretations, and open to being questioned and corrected? Or is it, as God's Word, perfect, without error, with no real inconsistencies, and "totally true and trustworthy" in everything it says?

These questions are meant to represent the two sides in the "battle for the Bible" that has consumed Christianity in North America for the last 125 years. The participants in this battle, the two sides, were known as modernists and fundamentalists in the first half of the twentieth century. More recently, the two sides have tended to use the designations "liberal" and "conservative."

This battle began in earnest in the United States in the 1880s, though it had been percolating in Europe long before. It began on this continent as "higher criticism" began to take root in American seminaries. Higher criticism, a part of the historical-critical method for studying the Bible, assumed that one could study the Bible like one might study any other ancient book, applying all the scientific and critical methods to this study. "Lower criticism" was the study of the ancient manuscripts of the Bible—there are thousands of them—with slight variants in them. Lower criticism is the detective work of reconstructing what the original manuscripts may have said, based upon a careful study of all of the variations in the ancient manuscripts. Every modern version of the Bible makes use of lower criticism in order to determine the best possible Hebrew and Greek text to use to translate the Bible into English.

> This battle [for the Bible] began in earnest in the United States in the 1880s, though it had been percolating in Europe long before. It began on this continent as "higher criticism" began to take root in American seminaries.

Higher criticism was focused on a careful study of the texts of the Bible to look for sources behind the documents as we have them. (For instance, it is generally agreed that Matthew, Mark, and Luke share common material, but who borrowed from whom, and did they have common sources they each used? And why, if they had common sources, do their stories at times disagree markedly from one another?) The Bible was often seen by higher critics as a merely human document that had undergone various revisions over time, as was true of many other ancient books. More radical higher critics questioned the authorship of virtually all of the books of the Bible, and determined that many were written long after the events described in the books, and that they may have included a significant amount of material that was not historical at all. In other words, much of the Bible was thought, by the radical higher critics, to be mythological in nature. This, in turn, called into question virtually every doctrine of the Christian faith.

In reaction to higher criticism, it is not difficult to imagine the next swing of the pendulum: fundamentalism. Fundamentalism involved a complete rejection of much of higher criticism, and an affirmation that the Bible was a different kind of book altogether, and not subject to the kind of criticism brought to bear on other ancient books. The Bible was said to be fully inspired by God, with every word placed in the minds of the biblical authors by God's Spirit (a view called "verbal, plenary inspiration"). Further, the fundamentalists claimed that since God authored the Bible, and God does not lie, nor is God ever in error, the Bible must be "inerrant," without error. Since lower criticism had already revealed the many variations in the text of the Bible as we have them, inerrancy was reserved for the "original autographs," the first writings of the biblical documents—documents that no one now possesses.

> In reaction to higher criticism, it is not difficult to imagine the next swing of the pendulum: fundamentalism. Fundamentalism involved a complete rejection of much of higher criticism, and an affirmation that the Bible was a different kind of book altogether, and not subject to the kind of criticism brought to bear on other ancient books.

So, this was the next great schism in the modern Christian church, and though it started in the Protestant churches, it crossed into the Roman Catholic Church as well. As already noted, this division has gone by several names over the last 150 years, but in the first half of the last century the two poles in the divide were known as "fundamentalists" and "modernists." The modernists embraced the historical-critical method for studying the Scriptures. Some were quite radical in their conclusions. Most were more moderate, holding to traditional Christianity, but willing to ask questions of the faith and remain open to new insights. Fundamentalists, as the other side came to be known, sought to ensure that their churches were not jettisoning what they considered the historical essentials of the Christian faith, including what became known as the five fundamentals of the faith: the inspiration of the Bible (as defined by the doctrine of inerrancy), the virgin birth, the atonement, the bodily resurrection of Jesus, and the reality of Jesus' miracles.

This division began with the nature of the Bible and how it was to be interpreted. It spread to theological issues. Ultimately, it also was manifest in the church's understanding of its mission. The fundamentalists tended to focus on evangelism and "winning" people to Christ, while the modernists would embrace and pursue the social gospel with its heady visions of societal transformation.

In many ways today's culture wars reflect the continuing battle between the modernists and the fundamentalists.

Many (most?) of today's conservatives continue to teach that "the Bible alone, and the Bible in its entirety, is the Word of God written and is therefore inerrant in the autographs."[3] Some conservatives continue to reject any insights gained from the application of the historical-critical method. The most conservative take a very literal reading of the Scriptures, affirming a creation that occurred in the last ten thousand years, rejecting the idea of women serving in leadership in the church, and affirming a belief that whatever the Bible says must be true and accurate on any matter it touches—science and history as much as theology and faith. Conservatives typically feel compelled to uphold the traditional claims of authorship even when an author's name is not specifically given within the text of the book (for instance, Matthew, Mark, and Luke are all anonymous works). A common battle cry of the conservative regarding the Bible might be "the Bible says it. I believe it. That settles it."

Today's more radical liberals continue to view most of the traditional claims of authorship in the Bible with great skepticism, and they question most traditional theological formulations drawn from the Scriptures. A recent example of this more radical liberal position would be the Jesus Seminar, in which a number of New Testament scholars met periodically to vote on which of the sayings in the Gospels might actually have been spoken by Jesus, rather than placed on his lips by the early church. The conclusions of the group were that only 18 percent of the words attributed to Jesus in the Gospels were likely actually spoken by him!

My Old Testament professor seemed obliged to teach us that this theory was "of course" not accurate, and that Moses was "really" the author of these books. But I remember thinking at the time that he didn't seem convinced of this himself, but instead was giving us the "acceptable" view. He taught us the arguments used to refute the documentary hypothesis, but I remember thinking, "Wait a minute; this theory makes some sense to me."

As a result of these and similar investigations, some have rejected virtually every part of the traditional theological formulations of the Christian faith.

Most Christians find themselves between these two poles of the most conservative and most liberal Christians. Many conservatives today are willing to embrace, with caution, some of the methods and conclusions of higher criticism. When I attended Oral Roberts University, I was taught these methodologies and many of their less radical conclusions. It was there that I was first exposed to the "documentary hypothesis"—the idea that Moses did not write the first five books of the Bible as traditionally thought, but rather that they came from at least four separate sources whose work was pieced together by later editors. My Old Testament professor seemed obliged to teach us that this theory was "of course" not accurate, and that Moses was "really" the author of these books. But I remember thinking at the time that he didn't seem convinced of this himself, but instead was giving us the "acceptable" view. He taught us the arguments used to refute the documentary hypothesis, but I remember thinking, "Wait a minute; this theory makes some sense to me."

Likewise, many self-described liberals find the conclusions of the Jesus Seminar absurd, and embrace most of the Synoptic Gospels' depictions of Jesus' teachings as being at least inspired by actual sayings of Jesus. Many of the persons I know who consider themselves liberal would also affirm the five "fundamentals" put forth in 1910 (rejecting inerrancy, but otherwise affirming that the Holy Spirit inspired, in some way, the Scriptures, that Jesus was born of a virgin, that Christ died for the sins of the world, that he bodily rose from the dead, and that he worked miracles).[4] They would reject a literalistic reading of the Bible, embrace a willingness to ask questions and an openness to the possibility that not everything recorded in the Gospels is strictly historical.

It was a great blessing for me to attend and study the Bible at a more conservative undergraduate school and then to attend and study the Bible at a more liberal theological seminary. These two perspectives have fundamentally shaped my faith and under-

I find that when I'm reading conservative commentaries I am always asking critical questions of them. And when I am reading liberal commentaries, I find I am always critiquing the more radical claims from a conservative perspective.

standing of the Bible. I find that when I'm reading conservative commentaries, I am always asking critical questions of them. And when I am reading liberal commentaries, I find I am always critiquing the more radical claims from a conservative perspective.

When studying for sermons, I will have open before me the more traditional *NIV Study Bible* and the more progressive *New Interpreter's Bible*. I have in my library commentaries that are written by conservatives and progressives. Among my "hermeneutical" principles (interpretive principles) is that I am open to question any doctrine or biblical text, but the weight of evidence must be overwhelmingly strong in order to overturn more traditional affirmations about the authorship of this or that scripture, or of a particular interpretation of Scripture, and this is particularly true when it comes to the doctrinal affirmations of the early church. I have always held onto something I was taught in college by a wise professor (who likely borrowed it from someone else): "All that is old may not be gold, but all that is new is not necessarily true"!

Liberals have had a tendency to focus on the Bible's humanity. They assume (rightly so, I think) that every biblical author had an agenda, and brought to their work certain presuppositions and theological and cultural understandings, just as any of us do when we write. They were not perfect people. They each had their own character, their own biases, their own experiences, and a particular situation they were writing out of. Likewise, their intended readers were living

All that is old may not be gold, but all that is new is not necessarily true!

in a particular historical situation, and had a history, and a character, and biases, which are all factored into what the author was writing. With this bias toward the Bible's humanity, the challenge for the liberal is to determine how the Bible is, in any meaningful sense, the "word of God" and how it functions as an authority in one's life and for the church.

If the liberals tend to emphasize the Bible's humanity at the expense of its divinity, the conservatives often emphasize the Bible's divinity at the expense of its humanity. To many nonconservatives, conservative Christians appear to have elevated the Bible to be a fourth member of the Trinity. While the ancient creeds all started with the affirmation of belief in God, many conservative churches and parachurch ministries begin

If the liberals tend to emphasize the Bible's humanity at the expense of its divinity, the conservatives often emphasize the Bible's divinity at the expense of its humanity. To many nonconservatives, conservative Christians appear to have elevated the Bible to be a fourth member of the Trinity.

their faith statements with an affirmation concerning the Bible. This seems strange to liberals and centrist Christians alike. The affirmation of the Bible's inerrancy feels to many Christians who do not hold this view to be a doctrine that is neither explicitly taught in the Scriptures, nor substantiated by the actual phenomena of the Bible.[5] Any serious-minded atheist can pick apart this doctrine with example after example of errors or inconsistencies in the Bible. It appears to liberals as though conservatives, out of fear and in an attempt to safeguard their faith from questioning, have developed a doctrine that effectively backs them into a corner. Many Christians believe the doctrine of inerrancy actually undermines the beauty and inspiration of the Scriptures. The Bible's humanity helps us make sense of the Bible's more difficult passages, both the inconsistencies[6] and, even more important, its words about God that seem grossly out of character for the God revealed in Jesus Christ.[7]

For many serious Christians who study the Scriptures, inerrancy actually becomes a stumbling block to their faith. I think of Bart Ehrman, professor of religious studies at the University of North Carolina and a *New York Times* bestselling author. He came to faith in a fundamentalist church, attended Moody Bible Institute and Wheaton College (both conservative Christian schools), and then pursued his master of divinity and PhD degrees at Princeton, focusing on New Testament studies. His faith had been built upon a conservative understanding of the Scriptures. But the more he studied the Bible, both its content and its formation, the more untenable inerrancy became to him. And when that understanding of the Bible was no longer tenable, his faith, which was built upon the premise of inerrancy, was no longer tenable either. Today Ehrman writes extensively on the Bible, but considers himself an agnostic. A significant number of former fundamentalists have left the faith or migrated to more liberal churches as a result of their inability to reconcile the Scriptures, as we have them, with the doctrine of inerrancy upon which they had built their faith.

So, while the liberals may err on the side of overemphasizing the Bible's humanity while neglecting its divinity, conservatives may err on the side of overemphasizing the Bible's divinity while negating its humanity. Once again the truth and place of balance seems to be somewhere in the gray between these two.

I appreciate Rob Bell's summary of his experience of the Bible in his book *Velvet Elvis*: "I continue to find the Bible the most mysterious book—the more insight I gain, the more I realize how much I don't know. It inspires and encourages, and it also frustrates and provokes. The Bible is a difficult book." [8] It *is* a difficult and complex book. But it is also a wonderful, amazing, and life-giving book.

So, what is the Bible? It is a book written by people who lived in ancient times, with their own biases and limitations in knowledge, who had great insights and experiences of God, yet who were also capable of misunderstandings, inconsistencies, and writing things that may have been important to their first readers, but not necessarily timeless words that apply in every situation. *And* it is a book through which God has spoken and still speaks, one that is "living and active" and through which God comforts, challenges, and inspires, the very reading of which has the power to change lives.

It is a book through which God has spoken and still speaks, one that is "living and active," and through which God comforts, challenges, and inspires, the very reading of which has the power to change lives.

An analogy that I have found helpful in thinking about the Bible is the Eucharist or Holy Communion. When it comes to the bread and wine Christians receive in Holy Communion, we know that human hands created these things. In our church, Great Harvest Bread Company prepares the wheat bread we use in the Eucharist. Most Methodists use unfermented wine, or grape juice (Dr. Welch was a Methodist who perfected the process of pasteurizing grape juice, in part for this purpose).

We can analyze the ingredients that go into the bread and the wine. And we can describe the production process that formed them. We know who pours the wine and cuts the bread for Holy Communion. All this is done by human hands.

But something happens to this bread and wine as people come forward to receive it during Holy Communion. The Holy Spirit uses the bread and wine as an instrument by which grace is imparted. People come to the Lord's table as an expression of their faith. They come seeking to meet Christ in the breaking of the bread and the sharing of the cup. This meal becomes holy, as they receive it. They see in it the suffering and death of Christ. As they eat it they receive, in tangible form, the grace of God. I see in their eyes tears of joy, relief, or hope, as they receive this meal. Therefore, while the bread and wine are made by human hands, in the communion meal they become instruments of Christ, in which he reveals himself, extends his grace, and touches their hearts.

I see the Bible in much the same way. It is a kind of Eucharist, written by human beings, shaped by their historical context, their limitations, and their agendas, yet used by God, despite its imperfections, in a sacramental way. Through the Bible, God imparts grace and wisdom, truth and hope. As we approach it, listening carefully for God to speak, this book teaches, and reproves, corrects, and trains us so that we are ready to do God's work.

I believe we must say yes to biblical criticism, to bringing the best of human scholarship to analyzing and dissecting and studying the text and yes to asking questions. We don't have to be afraid of this. We don't have to be afraid to discover the Bible's humanity. We don't have to hide it, harmonize it, or explain it away. And we must say yes to reading, studying, meditating, and demonstrating great respect for this book, as we listen for God's voice in its words.

> We don't have to be afraid to discover the Bible's humanity. We don't have to hide it, harmonize it, or explain it away.

I love the Bible like no other book. None other has so shaped my thoughts, my values, my life. Its story has become my story. Each day as I open and read it I feel connected to God, and find my soul nourished by it. I want to live by its precepts—to allow its words to be a "lamp to my feet and a light to my path" (Psalm 119:105). I love *both* its humanity and its divinity. Both make it what it is. I think this balance is what the great Methodist theologian Albert Outler had in mind when he wrote:

> In almost any foreseeable future, Christianity will "disciple all the nations" more effectively, as it is enabled to summon more and more open-hearted interpreters . . . to hands-on

engagements with the Bible. . . . In response, inquiring souls may stand *before* the Scriptures—not *under* them in mindless assent; not *above* them, in hermeneutical arrogance—to see and hear what may be seen and heard of the Mystery of the Lord Almighty.[9]

Notes

1. Zachary Forrest y Salazar, "Christians, Gray Areas, and Biblical Dynamics," at www.johnnybeloved.com—a website worth reading.
2. Note that this chapter begins with a bit of the history of the battles over the Bible and its content may seem a bit tedious to you. I would encourage you to read on nonetheless. The battle over the Bible is at the crux of the culture wars and "black and whiteness" of Christianity today. In this chapter I will offer the beginning of a way forward.
3. Evangelical Theological Society, "F.A.Q.," www.etsjets.org/?q=faq.
4. Here Karl Barth and later theologians like Pannenberg were helpful in leading younger liberals to reconsider the historic doctrines of the faith.
5. The Chicago Statement on Inerrancy, one of the definitive statements by the proponents of this view, tells us that we should not worry about whether the Bible actually appears inerrant; we are to "honor" God by accepting this doctrine by faith *even though the Bible does not appear to actually be inerrant.*
6. Many conservative Christians gloss over the inconsistencies in the Bible. For just one example, take a few minutes to read each of the four Gospel accounts of the resurrection. On a sheet of paper make four columns, one for each Gospel account, and then note the details of each account and their differences and similarities. They agree regarding the most important detail—that Jesus rose from the grave—but they have differences that are difficult to reconcile without doing damage to each Gospel writer's account. This is only one of hundreds of examples throughout the Bible.
7. This is the perennial problem encountered by any thoughtful person who reads the Bible. How can God seem so bloodthirsty, vengeful, and unjust in certain passages in the Old Testament (1 Samuel 15 and his command of the extermination of the Amalekites is but one of many examples) while gracious and merciful in so many others? How could the God of the parable of the Prodigal Son, who cries from the cross "Father forgive them," be the same God who says in Deuteronomy 32:41b-42 (NIV), "I will take vengeance on my adversaries and repay those who hate me. I will make my arrows drunk with blood, while my sword devours flesh"? Did God change, or did humanity gain a deeper and clearer understanding of God? The latter is possible

if we reject the idea that every word of Scripture was chosen by God and is "totally true and trustworthy."

8. Rob Bell, *Velvet Elvis: Repainting the Christian Faith* (Grand Rapids: Zondervan, 2005), 41.

9. Albert C. Outler, "Toward a Postliberal Hermeneutics," *Theology Today* 42, no. 3 (October 1985): 281-91.

Nine
The Galileo Affair

*We say, pronounce, sentence, and declare, that thou, the
said Galileo, by the things deduced during this trial, and by thee
confessed as above, hast rendered thyself vehemently suspected
of heresy by this Holy Office, that is, of having believed and held a
doctrine which is false, and contrary to the Holy Scriptures, to wit:
that the Sun is the centre of the universe, and that it does not move
from east to west, and that the Earth moves and is not the centre of
the universe: and that an opinion may be held and defended as
probable after having been declared and defined as contrary to
Holy Scripture; and in consequence thou hast incurred all the
censures and penalties of the Sacred Canons, and other Decrees
both general and particular, against such offenders imposed and
promulgated.*

*— Report of the Tribunal of the Supreme Inquisition,
June 22, 1633*

Galileo Galilei is among the most important scientists who has
ever lived. Born in 1564 in Pisa, Italy, his work as a mathe-
matician, astronomer, inventor, and philosopher continues to influence science to this day. In church circles he will always be a
source of embarrassment. In June of 1633 the sixty-nine-year-old
Galileo was convicted of heresy for promulgating the idea that the
earth revolves around the sun. This was not a new idea, and in
many ways Galileo was advocating the already rejected arguments
of Copernicus, who died twenty years before Galileo was born.

The church noted that not only did Galileo's theory contradict a long line of scientists, his teaching that the earth was not the
center of our solar system, and consequently not the center of the

universe, flew in the face of several passages of Scripture as well. The result was that Galileo was brought before the Roman Catholic Church's Inquisition. After he was found guilty, the inquisitors showed mercy upon Galileo, allowing him to be absolved of his sin if he would admit the error of his ways and agree not to teach this theory again. Galileo read a statement formally repenting of what he had taught—presumably with fingers crossed behind his back as he did so.

This is the place to begin a discussion of the relationship between science and religion. We must be clear about the mistake the church made here and be careful not to repeat it. The mistake of the church was not that it believed that the earth was the center of the universe and that the sun revolved around it. Nearly everyone in that day believed this, whether they believed in God or not. It was a view held by Aristotle, Ptolemy, and nearly every other great philosopher and scientist up to this time. And it was a view that lined up with common sense. From the vantage point of any human being, the earth appears to be stationary and appears to be at the center of the universe, with the sun and all other celestial bodies moving while we stand still. To this day we speak of the sun rising and the sun setting. Rather than the church's big mistake, this was an excusable error.

> When it comes to the tension that exists between science and religion, one incident stands out as the tragic beginning point for much of that tension: the Galileo affair.

The church's big mistakes were failing to understand the relationship between science and the Bible, judging a scientific theory based upon a literal reading of Scripture, and believing that it was the church's role to judge and approve or disapprove of scientific theories.

To ask the Bible to function as a scientific textbook is to fundamentally misunderstand the intention of the Scriptures. I believe that God delights in allowing us to explore the workings of

To ask the Bible to function as a scientific textbook is to fundamentally misunderstand the intention of the Scriptures.

his universe. God gave us a gift of curiosity, and God takes pleasure in our studying, exploring, and trying to understand his creation.

When I was a boy I remember seeing, for the first time, a ship inside a bottle. Its owner took great delight in showing it to me, and even more delight in my intense desire to know how the ship got inside the bottle. He did not tell me the answer when I first asked him. He made me think about the question. He forced me to analyze the possible solutions. It was not just a game to him; it was an exercise in teaching me to think carefully, and to solve problems. Finally, he helped me "discover" the secret to how the boat came to be inside the bottle—and here, too, he took delight.

I wonder if this is not a picture of why God does not reveal the knowledge of the universe to us through a book of physics, a book of chemistry, and a book of astronomy. Again, God takes delight in our curiosity, and in our attempts at discovery. God knew that one day human beings would learn that the earth revolves around the sun. God did not need to correct the cosmology of the biblical authors who thought it was the other way around. This further reminds us that the Bible was written to reveal who God is, and to teach us something about ourselves. It was not written to reveal the fundamental laws of physics, chemistry, or biology.

Unfortunately, the Galileo incident came to represent the relationship between some leading scientists and religion for the next five hundred years. Up to the time of Galileo, religion and science were partners in a quest for knowledge. Following this time they were seen as being at odds with each other—a mutual threat one to the other.

Both science and religion are interested in knowledge and truth. Some time ago I sat down with Dr. Brendan Sweetman, the chair of the department of philosophy at Rockhurst University in Kansas City, Missouri. He has degrees from University College

Dublin, Ireland, and a PhD from the University of Southern California. He is a prolific writer and one of his interests is the issue of science and religion. I asked him what he saw as the work of science and the work of religion. He replied:

> Science can help us to understand the physical realm, religion helps us understand the ultimate questions, and they both work together to understand reality. . . . Some would say that science is atheistic because it excludes any supernatural explanations. But this is not true. Its method excludes appealing to supernatural explanations. . . . It can't explain things like morality, the soul, consciousness, and all of those issues that have been closely related to religion.

Here we might remember a quote often attributed to Galileo, when he was making the case that his new views of the earth rotating around the sun were not contradictory to the Christian faith. He said, "The Bible teaches men how to go to heaven, not how the heavens go."

The Bible teaches men how to go to heaven, not how the heavens go.

Take for example the piano. Science will help us understand everything there is to know about a piano, down to its subatomic structure. At a very simple level, scientists can explain to us how striking a key causes a hammer to strike a set of strings, which produces a sound wave. The scientist will help us understand how that sound wave travels through space. Neuroscientists can tell us what happens when one of those sound waves enters your ear, ultimately sending electrical impulses to the brain, which then translates them into sound.

But while this explanation of how the piano works is scientifically accurate, it doesn't begin to explain what happens when we hear a Mozart sonata played on the piano, or, if you prefer, the cool sounds of jazz pianist Dave Brubeck, or the soothing sounds of Jim Brickman. Science can only explain the mechanics. Religion explains that we are creatures with souls, that music is in part a gift from God, that it speaks to us and touches us, as does art and worship and prayer and a host of other things—because there is more to us than meets the eye.

Science, without God, reminds me of a docent at the Sistine Chapel talking nonstop about the chemical make-up of the pigmentation in the frescoes, while never really helping me appreciate the amazing images in the ceiling, or Michelangelo, who painted them. It is like a biochemist telling me that the love I feel for my wife is really a function of oxytocin flooding my brain when we embrace. My answer would be "Yes, but . . ."

Last year for Christmas my wife, knowing my interest in the stars, bought me a Celestron SkyScout. This is an amazing device that utilizes global positioning satellites to identify stars and planets in the night sky. I point it at a star, center the star in the viewfinder, and hit the "identify" button. Over the headset I receive a recorded message telling me about the star I'm looking at. I love this device!

Recently, I walked outside without my SkyScout. It was a moonless night and the skies were dark. I live in the country, and there are no streetlights in my neighborhood. And when I looked up at the sky—I'm not exaggerating—it simply took my breath away. I could see the Milky Way above me. Orion was climbing in the southeastern sky, and the Pleiades, and Cassiopeia and the Big Dipper were all there. And I could not help myself—I stood there in the darkness, hands upraised, and I began to recite those ancient words, written three thousand years ago by another stargazer:

The heavens are telling the glory of God;
    and the firmament proclaims his handiwork.
Day to day pours forth speech,
    and night to night declares knowledge. (Psalm 19:1-2)

Between the black-and-whiteness of the conflict between science and religion is a place where both are valued for what they offer us as human beings: a place where we don't have to choose between science and religion. They are not adversaries, but two different ways of helping us understand the universe and our place in it. Those who recognize this have come to appreciate the value of gray.

> Science and religion are not adversaries, but two different ways of helping us understand the universe and our place in it.

T e n
Apes, Evolution, Adam and Eve

So God created humankind in his image, in the image of God
he created them; male and female he created them. . . . God saw
everything that he had made, and indeed, it was very good. And
there was evening and there was morning, the sixth day.
—Genesis 1:27, 31

F ew issues have received as much attention in the culture wars
as the concern over human origins and the teaching of evolution. Most recently, the battles over teaching evolution have been
revived by the rise of those advocating the teaching of Intelligent
Design alongside evolution in the public schools. Where this has
not succeeded there have been attempts to force teachers or text-
books to indicate that evolution is only a theory. In this chapter
we'll consider the theory of evolution and three possible Christian responses to it.

Understanding the Theory of Evolution

The word *evolution* simply signifies change over time. We see
evolution all around us. Everything changes over time. As we look
back over the history of planet Earth, it seems clear that this planet
has been marked by change. From the simplest unicellular life
forms to the rise of more complex forms and the extinction of others, and ultimately the arrival of human beings, life on Earth has
been constantly changing. The idea of change over time is a fact
everyone acknowledges. When we speak of the theory of evolution, however, we're speaking of a particular model for explaining
those changes over time. Charles Darwin's theory of evolution by

natural selection proposes a way of explaining the mechanics of the changes we find in the fossil record. It proposes that simpler life forms actually changed, over time, to become more complex life forms.

Darwin's theory was published in 1859 as *On the Origin of Species by Means of Natural Selection*. His was a revolutionary idea that has profoundly shaped scientific and sociological thought ever since. What does the theory of evolution by natural selection teach? It proposes that all forms of life on earth evolved from simpler life forms, and that the mechanism for that evolution begins with mutation. Some time ago I sat down with Dr. Colin Barnstable, a professor of neurobiology at the Yale University School of Medicine, whose PhD is in genetics. I asked if he could offer a simple explanation of how Darwin's theory works. He said:

> Darwin's theory of evolution has three components: the first is *mutation*—a series of changes in the chemistry of the genetic DNA. Mutation happens in all organisms. Mutation leads to *variation*. The final point of evolution is *selection*. In any given environment there are certain variations that are advantageous and others that are not. Those that are advantageous may be passed on to offspring, and these offspring may have a competitive advantage over others that do not possess the variation. Over long periods of time an increasing number of variations can result in entirely new species. This is the process of natural selection.
>
> Darwin suggested that this process could explain the development of all life forms on earth—that each life form was the result of a long history of small changes or mutations and the environmental factors favoring certain mutations and selecting against others. Those traits that allowed a given life form to reproduce more effectively or frequently were passed on. Over time, the cumulative effect of these small changes led to the development of entire new species and increasingly better-suited organisms that were capable of surviving in different environments.

So what's all the fuss about this theory? It seems harmless enough to many, and even brilliant or self-evident to others. Why would so many Christians (and I might add Muslims and a few others) find this theory difficult to accept? There are no doubt many reasons. I'll offer four.

The primary reason some Christians have struggled with evolution is that it contradicts a literal reading of the creation story in Genesis 1. Some read the Genesis account of creation as history, and thus believe that God created everything from nothing in six twenty-four-hour days. Evolution is impossible to reconcile with this reading of Genesis.

Second, some Christians believe that evolutionary theory diminishes (if it does not eliminate outright) the role of God in creation. If the development of life happened by mutation, adaptation, and natural selection, what role did God play in creation?

Third, some Christians believe that if human beings evolved from other forms of life—if we shared a common ancestor with apes (or sea sponges, for that matter)—what does that say about humans? On many occasions I've heard people protest the theory of evolution by saying things like "My grandpa wasn't an ape!"

Each of the first three objections to evolution offered by Christians can be overcome, and thus allow a Christian to accept evolution, in my mind, the fourth might be a "deal killer." And the fourth depends upon how evolution is defined.

In 1995 the National Association of Biology Teachers included in their teaching materials about evolution a statement that they believed accurately reflected the truth about the theory of evolution. This is the statement as it appeared in 1995:

> The diversity of life on earth is the outcome of evolution: an *unsupervised, impersonal,* unpredictable and natural process of temporal descent with genetic modification that is affected by natural selection, chance, historical contingencies and changing environments. (emphasis added)[1]

The sticking point is the assertion that life on earth is the result of an unsupervised and impersonal (sometimes "unplanned" is added) process. To suggest that creation has occurred without supervision and that it was impersonal is to exclude any role for God in creation. If this is what the scientist is asking people of faith to believe, I cannot accept this, and this statement cannot be reconciled with the Bible or Christian theology. *I will also say that this statement is bad science*—it is bad

> The sticking point is the assertion that life on earth is the result of an unsupervised, impersonal (sometimes "unplanned" is added) process.

science because it draws a conclusion about how evolution works that goes beyond what science can speak to. To say that the diversity of life is the result of an unsupervised, impersonal process is to make a statement about religion and philosophy—it is to exclude the possibility that God is at work in this process or that God is supervising this process. A handful of scientists have gone further with their statements about evolution. Edward Wilson writes: "No species, ours included, possesses a purpose beyond the imperatives created by its genetic history."[2] And George Gaylord Simpson has stated: "Man is the result of a purposeless and natural process that did not have him in mind."[3] Richard Dawkins notes that the universe has "no design, no purpose, no evil and no good, nothing but blind, pitiless indifference."[4] This is not a scientific statement of fact—it is a philosophical statement that is irreconcilable not only with Christianity but also with nearly every theistic religion in the world.

The question becomes: Is this the definition of evolution? Does evolution necessarily require that the process be unsupervised and impersonal? I would suggest that evolution describes a mechanism, not a philosophy, and that there are many who embrace evolution who believe that the evolutionary process was supervised by God, planned and designed by God, and filled with purpose beyond simply the propagation of species.

The National Association of Biology Teachers, after having been challenged on its language, recognized that the inclusion of the words *impersonal* and *unsupervised* made speculative philosophical statements and were not intrinsic to the definition of evolution. It removed them from its definition of evolution in its teaching materials beginning in 1997.

Having understood why some Christians struggle with evolution, let's look at three of the dominant responses that Christians have made to evolution.

Creation Science

Not long ago, I attended a meeting of young earth Creation scientists in Kansas City. I was curious as to what the folks were like who were championing this view. There were probably fifty people gathered in a small fundamentalist church, led by the head of the organization—an amiable and very passionate man who enjoyed lecturing and seeking to make the case for a young earth and a literal reading of the creation account in Genesis. He repeatedly referred to the Genesis account as the "historical record" composed by the only One who was actually present for the creation: God. The position these folks advocate is known as Creation Science, or Scientific Creationism. Creation scientists begin their work with a belief that the earth is less than ten thousand years old, a belief that is drawn, at least in part, by stringing together the chronologies found in the Old Testament. Many believe that everything that exists was created in six twenty-four-hour periods and that the flood described in the Bible occurred around five thousand years ago and can explain the fossil record, the apparent ice ages, and the formation of the various continents.[5] With this as their starting point they develop theories as to how the data from nature can be made to fit into these parameters.[6] It is easy to underestimate this group, or to dismiss its members as uninformed. But the faculty of the Institute for Creation Research includes eight PhDs in geology, astrophysics, biochemistry, and biology. They have begun with a presupposition based upon their faith regarding the age of the earth and the way in which creation took place, and then they bring their best scientific training to bear in seeking to reconcile the geological and biological data with the

Genesis story of creation. The theories they have proposed are quite interesting, though I find them unconvincing.

Intelligent Design

A second Christian response to evolution is what today is called Intelligent Design. Intelligent Design proponents look at evolution and disagree with its basic premise—they are not arguing that the earth is less than ten thousand years old. They don't even disagree that some of the principles of Darwin's theory are correct. They are not trying to make science fit a literal reading of Genesis. But they look at what we can observe in the physical world, particularly the complexity we see in life, and they believe this cannot adequately be explained by evolution.

> The claim of Intelligent Design is that there are features of the natural world that can best be explained by Intelligence.

One of the proponents of Intelligent Design, and a director of Intelligent Design Network in Kansas City, is Dr. Bill Harris. Harris is the Daniel J. Lauer Professor of Metabolism and Vascular Research at the University of Missouri at Kansas City School of Medicine and the codirector of the Saint Luke's Hospital Lipid and Diabetes Research Center. He has published eighty-nine scientific articles in peer-reviewed journals, he's a reviewer in a host of major journals, and he's received numerous awards for his work. I sat down with him and asked him to tell me about Intelligent Design and this is what he said.

> The claim of Intelligent Design is that there are features of the natural world that can best be explained by Intelligence. An example is the code of DNA—we know of no codes that did not come out of a mind. That is the icon of Intelligent Design. We see information in nature that nothing can explain other than Intelligence. . . . Evolution claims that life in all its diversity is a result of an unplanned process, and Intelligent Design

disagrees with that point of view. We believe that there is evidence in biology, cosmology, in the natural world for the interaction with an Intelligence, both for its origin and its development and that there are some pieces of the creation that call out for a Creator. . . . To me the central question of this whole argument is Is it guided or is it unguided? It is not the age of the earth. . . . Anything that fits with a guided process a theist can be happy with. There's a famous quote by Richard Dawkins that says "Evolution made it possible to be an intellectually satisfied atheist." I think Intelligent Design made it possible to be an intellectually satisfied theist. The data of science is pointing to a design—a plan.

Discussion of Intelligent Design has highlighted the amazing complexity of life and raised questions about whether evolution alone is sufficient to explain this complexity, and it has given an opportunity for a number of scientists to speak of their faith in a God who was involved in lending a helping hand in creation and the formation of life on this planet. I am inclined to agree with the Intelligent Design folks in finding it difficult to imagine that science can adequately explain how the entire cosmos sprang forth from an initial "bang" or that all life spontaneously developed in the primordial soup of this earth. Dawkins himself noted that the likelihood of this happening was akin to a tornado blowing through a metal scrap yard, and leaving behind a perfectly formed Boeing jet in its wake. [7]

On another note, I might mention that one of the women in my congregation told me she struggled a bit with Intelligent Design. She said, "Anyone who has ever met my husband would have a tough time believing in Intelligent Design!" Her husband and I both had a good laugh.

Theistic Evolution

This brings us to our third type of response of Christians to evolution. There are Christians who look at evolutionary theory and believe it makes sense as a mechanism describing the changes we see in life forms in the fossil record, and the development of the millions of life forms we see on our planet today. Like those who support Intelligent Design, these reject the idea that evolution is unsupervised, impersonal, unplanned, or purpose-less. They embrace evolution, but see evolution itself as designed by

B. B. Warfield, known as one of the fathers of biblical inerrancy— the cornerstone of modern fundamentalism—embraced theistic evolution.

God and as his plan for calling forth life. They note that the Bible tells us that God spoke and life developed, and that all life came from the earth. But regarding *how* God did this, the Bible is silent. These Christians believe evolution explains the process by which God brought about life from the dust of the earth. They do not see evolution as a threat to the Christian faith, nor do they believe that Christianity and evolution are mutually exclusive ideas.

Lest you think this is only a view that liberals hold, you'll find that Evangelicals, Roman Catholics, mainline Protestants,

Just as we might want to consider that God created the laws that gave rise to the universe, I think a God who created the laws that govern evolution is magnificent. It doesn't deny the role of God at all.

and even a few fundamentalists hold this view. Most notable among fundamentalists who accepted evolution was B. B. Warfield, known as one of the fathers of biblical inerrancy— the cornerstone of modern fundamentalism. He did not see embracing evolution as inconsistent with his understanding of the inerrancy of Scripture.

When I asked Dr. Barnstable, the Yale neurobiologist, if he believed that evolution was incompatible with Christian faith, he responded:

I certainly don't think they are incompatible. Evolution describes a process. Yes it does contradict the simplest interpretation of Genesis, but I don't think it necessarily excludes a role for God. As we understand evolution, there is such an elegance, we can marvel at this process. Just as we might want to consider that God created the laws that gave rise to the universe, I think a God which created the laws which govern evolution is magnificent. It doesn't deny the role of God at all.

There's a lot of black-and-white thinking in the area of human origins. The creation scientists can't move beyond a literal reading of Genesis. Some evolutionists are convinced that evolution can lead us to the knowledge that there is no God and that human life is simply the result of random mutations with no purpose, and no Creator. Both of these views fail to see that Genesis and Darwin are not mutually exclusive. They fail to see the gray.

Like the nineteenth-century scholar Benjamin Warfield, and a host of others, I find the theory of evolution quite compelling as a way of explaining the mechanism or process by which life adapted and changed, and became more complex, over the last four billion years. I believe in an Intelligent Designer whose purposeful plans created the conditions for life, and who,

> Evolution seems an elegant explanation of the mechanism God employed—the laws that he established to accomplish his purposes for creation.

I believe, did intervene at key places in the evolutionary development of life on our planet. Evolution seems an elegant explanation of the mechanism God employed—the laws that he established to accomplish his purposes for creation. I embrace evolution, but I also believe that there were places during the evolution of life on our planet where God may have played a more direct role in creation. The prime example may have been the moment when hominids became human—creatures with a higher consciousness, with a soul.

Evolution attempts to explain the process by which various life forms continued to develop, change, and adapt to their environment, resulting in greater complexity and more "fit" life forms. I find it a reasonable explanation for the development of the multitude of species on earth. It does not address the question of how the first life forms developed, which I believe to have been an act of God. Likewise, while evolution may be able to explain the development of intelligence, I don't think it is sufficient to explain the human soul. Evolution is not a threat to my faith, but it alone doesn't speak to our ultimate origins, or the purpose in creation, or the meaning of our lives, or what it means to be human. For this I turn to the Bible, particularly to the story of creation as found in the book of Genesis.

Notes

1. This statement, and its introductory paragraph, is quoted in "NABT Statement on Evolution Evolves," by Eugenie C. Scott at the National Center for Science Education website article dated May of 1998, www.ncseweb.org/resources/articles/8954_nabt_statement_on_evolution_ev_5_21_1998.asp, emphasis added.
2. Edward O. Wilson, *On Human Nature* (Cambridge, Mass.: Harvard University Press, 1978), 2.
3. George Gaylord Simpson, *The Meaning of Evolution*, rev. ed. (New Haven: New American Library, 1967), 345.
4. Richard Dawkins, *River Out of Eden* (New York: Basic, 1995), 133.
5. For a video showing how young earth Creationists understand the role of the biblical flood in creating fossils and continents, see www.mamouth.activnet works.net/samizdat.qc.ca/fontaine.mov.
6. See www.icr.org/creationscientists/biologicalscientists.html.
7. Richard Dawkins, *The God Delusion* (Boston: Houghton-Mifflin, 2006), 113.

Eleven
Is *Your* Jesus Too Small?

> *I first got acquainted with Jesus when I was a child, singing,*
> *"Jesus Loves Me" in Sunday school, addressing bedtime prayers to*
> *"Dear Lord Jesus" . . . I associated Jesus with Kool-Aid and sugar*
> *cookies and gold stars for good attendance. . . . Jesus, I [later]*
> *found, bore little resemblance to the Mister Rogers figure I had met*
> *in Sunday school, and was remarkably unlike the person I had*
> *studied in Bible college. For one thing he was far less tame.*
> —Philip Yancey[1]

In few places is the divide between "liberal" and "conservative" within the Christian faith more evident than in how each side understands the person of Jesus and what it means to be his disciples. Let's consider a few examples of these very different ways of seeing Jesus and the salvation that he brings.

Liberal Christians tend to focus on Jesus as a revolutionary, seeking to upend the social order, to lead people to justice and radical obedience to the will of God, and to usher in the reign of God. They cite the words of Jesus' first sermon, as recorded in Luke 4:18, where Jesus quotes Isaiah.

> "The Spirit of the Lord is upon me,
>   because he has anointed me
>   to bring good news to the poor.
> He has sent me to proclaim release to the captives
>   and recovery of sight to the blind,
>   to let the oppressed go free."

They focus on scriptures like Matthew 25:31-45, where the sole criterion of the Last Judgment is what we do or do not do for the poor and those in need (a passage, they note, that says nothing of "accepting Jesus as one's personal Lord and Savior"); or his footwashing with the disciples where Jesus demonstrates the role of radical servanthood. They highlight Jesus' call to love not only our neighbor but also our enemies. They see in the parable of the Good Samaritan, Christ's call to compassion and the breaking down of societal structures of racism and classism. They note that Jesus sought the outcasts and the underside of society. He invited women into his ministry, including those who were despised by society and used by men. He is the model for a prophet of social justice. He calls us to lay aside our sins of apathy toward those in need, our materialism, our bigotry, and to work for a world that looks more like the kingdom of God. Racism, injustice, poverty, war—these are the sins that tend to receive a bit more attention than others from liberals. Most liberal Christians would suggest that of our two political parties in the United States today, Jesus would be most inclined to be a Democrat.

Conservative Christians emphasize Jesus as "personal Savior and Lord." He is the one who expresses God's love to us individually, who came to seek and to save lost people, whose very name means *savior*, and who came to die for the sins of the world. He offered his life that we might be forgiven and made right with God. They tend to focus on Jesus' teaching that we must be "born again" and his words of invitation, "Come to me, all you that are weary and are carrying heavy burdens, and I will give you rest. Take my yoke upon you, and learn from me; for I am gentle and humble in heart, and you will find rest for your souls. For my yoke is easy, and my burden is light" (Matthew 11:28-30). For conservatives, Jesus' death on the cross was God's act to atone for the sins of the world. Jesus calls us to follow him in a life of personal holiness. For con-

> "Liberal" Christians tend to focus on Jesus as a revolutionary, seeking to upend the social order. Conservative Christians emphasize Jesus as "personal Savior and Lord."

servative Christians, being a Christian starts with having a "personal relationship" with Jesus—a relationship that changes our hearts. The world is changed as Christians tell others about Jesus and invite them to receive him. Jesus came to save us from our sins and to deliver us from hell. When it comes to societal ills, at least among white conservatives, the emphasis is typically on sexual sins and sexual purity. Abortion, homosexuality, and pornography are important topics. Since the 1980s, a large number of (again, predominantly white) conservative Christians have believed that if Jesus were a registered voter in America he would most certainly be a Republican.[2]

When I think of these two very different pictures of Jesus preached by the liberals and conservatives, I am reminded of J. B. Phillips's little book *Your God Is Too Small*. In the case of Jesus, when one accepts only the liberal or only the conservative portrayal of Jesus, I believe one comes away with a Jesus that is "too small." And neither the liberal nor the conservative view of Jesus seems entirely consistent with the Jesus we find in the Gospels.

Jesus was not a social reformer in the typical sense of the word. We may wish that he had taken on women's rights, and slavery, and oppression—but while his words and work would eventually lead his followers to push for reform in these areas, Jesus does not directly address them as a social reformer might. Jesus does not attack the pagan Roman Empire, but instead calls his disciples to pay their taxes, carry the packs of the soldiers if need be, and to turn the other cheek. He does not wage a war on poverty, though he calls his disciples to care for the hungry and sick and naked. His primary opponents were the religious leaders whom he condemned for their legalism and hypocrisy, rather than the wealthy or powerful in society.[3] Jesus invited people to love God and neighbor sacrificially.

Having said that, the *implications* of Jesus' call to

> Jesus was not a social reformer in the typical sense of the word. At the same time, Jesus never spoke about taking him "into your heart."

radical love and to the kingdom of God included all of the dimensions of social justice that liberals see in Jesus. Following him will lead us to care for the poor. It will lead us to love our neighbors sacrificially, regardless of the color of their skin. It will lead us to question the use of violence to solve problems. Following Jesus will lead us to build hospitals and clinics and homeless shelters and to pay attention to the weightier matters of the law: justice and mercy and faith (Matthew 25:23b). The very act of calling Jesus "Lord" was a revolutionary statement in a time when Caesar claimed that title for himself. Jesus was inviting people to a revolution of the heart and to live as citizens of God's kingdom.

At the same time, contrary to what my conservative friends preach, Jesus never speaks about taking him "into your heart." The concept of a personal relationship with Jesus for all future followers is hinted at but does not seem to be the essence of his message. Although he speaks about the afterlife, his comments about it are sparse. I believe he clearly sees himself atoning for the sins of the world[4] but this is only one dimension of his mission. The focus of his preaching and teaching is not to call people to a personal relationship with him or on saving us from our sin, but on calling people to repent and to submit to the reign of God. Every dimension of Jesus' ministry seemed focused on unpacking the implications of this for our lives. Yet, having said that, Jesus does speak of his death as bringing about the forgiveness of sins. In that most famous of all Gospel passages, John 3:16, we learn that "God so loved the world that he gave his only Son, so that everyone who believes in him may not perish but may have eternal life." And, particularly in John's Gospel, Jesus speaks about his followers having a relationship with him that is compared to a vine and its branches, and in which his believers share a certain unity with him.[5]

Jesus seemed to have little interest in the theological concerns of many evangelicals today. He did not lay out for us a systematic theology. He didn't clarify for us the issues of predestination or foreknowledge. He didn't seem concerned to lift up a doctrine of inerrancy of Scripture[6] or to teach us about justification by faith.

That's not to say that one can't find statements of Jesus that might be used to support these views, but they did not seem to be Jesus' primary concern. And though heaven and the afterlife are important,

Jesus preached one gospel that has, unfortunately, been truncated by the church into two: the social gospel and the personal evangelical gospel.

and Jesus clearly offers us hope for eternal life, he seems far more concerned with how we live in this life than the next.

So which Jesus are we to believe in and follow: the social reformer of liberal Christianity or the personal savior of conservative Christianity? Or, more to the point, is either of these portrayals of Jesus adequate apart from the other?

Jesus preached one gospel that has, unfortunately, been split by the church into two: the social gospel and the personal evangelical gospel. Neither gospel is complete apart from the other. Jesus invites us to be born again, calls us to take up our crosses and follow him, promises he will be with us always, offers us eternal life, and gives his life to save us from our sins. We can know Christ personally, talk with him, and be transformed by our love for him, *and* at the same time, Jesus calls us to yield our lives to God as King. He calls us to love our neighbor, and our neighbor is anyone who needs our love. That love is not a warm emotional bond, but a willingness to sacrifice what we have to meet the needs of the other. We are called to seek first not our own personal salvation and happiness, but the kingdom or reign of God. We are called to serve God, not money. We are to feed and clothe and shelter those in need. We are to heal the sick and to cast out the kind of demons we find destroying people today.

I fear that if Jesus came to our towns today, he would not sit for long in our churches. I suspect he might say, "You've totally missed the point! You've become Pharisees! Do you really think that this—what you're doing here—is why I suffered and died?" In more than a few of our churches, both liberal and conservative, I can imagine him standing and saying, "Woe to you, scribes and

I fear that if Jesus came to our towns today, he would not sit for long in our churches. I suspect he might say, "You've totally missed the point! You've become Pharisees! Do you really think that this—what you're doing here—is why I suffered and died?"

Pharisees, hypocrites! For you are like whitewashed tombs, which on the outside look beautiful, but inside they are full of the bones of the dead and of all kinds of filth. You've wounded the very people I came to love. On the day of judgment you will say to me, 'Lord, Lord, look at all we did for you,' but I will say to you, 'I never knew you!'" I wonder if most of us, myself included, would even recognize Jesus if he walked into our towns and churches today.

I think Jesus would find himself most comfortable sitting outside the homeless shelter or the gay bar, telling stories about prodigal children and the father who longs for them to come home. I can see him smiling as he tells about shepherds who won't stop looking for the sheep that wandered away. I can even picture him in the foyer (or food court?) of our contemporary *temples*—the shopping malls—saying things like, "Don't worry about what you will eat or drink or what you will wear . . . but seek first the kingdom of God and his righteousness," and "You cannot serve both God and money." I can picture him quietly entering the Oval Office, or the halls of Congress, to meet with all in power who claim to be his followers, and saying, "Let's talk about what I meant when I told you to love your enemy."

I can picture him quietly entering the Oval Office, or the halls of Congress, to meet with all in power who claim to be his followers, and saying, "Let's talk about what I meant when I told you to love your enemy."

Conservative and liberal conceptions of Jesus are "too small." It is only as we hold together these two pictures of the Master that Jesus and his call on our lives begins to come into clear focus. And it is only as we hold together both the evangelical and social gospels that we find the fullness of the good news. The evangelical gospel calls people to receive Jesus as Savior and to pursue a life of personal holiness. It offers the promise of grace, the love of God, a new beginning, and the hope of eternal life. The social gospel calls people to follow Jesus as Lord, and to live dangerously—even radically—in practicing his love toward others and pursuing the will of God in addressing issues of justice and mercy. It offers a life of meaning and an opportunity to change the world.

It is only as we hold together both the evangelical and social gospels that we find the fullness of the good news.

Finally, it is good to note that Jesus refused to fit anyone's mold. He shared things in common with several of the sects within Judaism of his day, but he found that none of them captured the fullness of the truth of the gospel. He challenged each of them. He challenged the Essenes and their extreme asceticism and their renunciation of the world. He challenged the Sadducees and their compromise with the world. He challenged the legalism and hypocrisy of the Pharisees. Each of these sects saw the world in black-and-white terms. Jesus drew elements from each of these sects, but his gospel refused to conform to any of their molds. He pushed them, challenged them, and ultimately alienated them, as he preached a gospel that appears to me to represent gray in a world of black and white.

Notes

1. Philip Yancey, *The Jesus I Never Knew* (Grand Rapids: Zondervan, 1995), 1, 15. Yancey is one of those Christians who seems to live very comfortably in the gray, and whose writings I always enjoy.
2. See George Hunter's book, *Christian, Evangelical & . . . Democrat?* (Nashville: Abingdon Press, 2006).

3. It could be argued that the religious leaders and the wealthy and powerful in society were one and the same, though this seems to be true primarily of the Sadducees, with whom Jesus seemed to have little to do. It is true that he commended Zacchaeus for giving away half of his income to the poor, and he told the rich young ruler to give away all of his income to the poor—but even Martin Luther King, Jr., did not believe this passage was a universal command that all of Christ's followers were to obey.

4. Some liberals question this, but his very name points to the idea of salvation. Forgiveness of sins is found as a part of his mission from the birth narratives forward. At the Last Supper Jesus clearly points in this direction. And his love for sinners seems to indicate that this was a major part of his mission.

5. See the vine and branches metaphor in John 15, and Jesus' priestly prayer in John 17.

6. In fact, Matthew 5:17-20, the one passage in which Jesus comes closest to this, related to the law, is one that is somewhat perplexing and requires a bit of creative exegesis on the part of conservatives. Jesus does not seem to think clarifying the hallmark doctrine of the reformation, justification by faith, was critical. In fact, his teachings tend to argue against this, particularly the parable of the sheep and the goats.

Twelve
Will There Be Hindus in Heaven?

> *I have never been able to conjure up (as some great Evangeli-*
> *cal missionaries have) the appalling vision of the millions who are*
> *not only perishing but will inevitably perish. On the other hand . . .*
> *I am not and cannot be a universalist. Between these extremes I*
> *cherish and hope that the majority of the human race will be saved.*
> *And I have a solid biblical basis for this belief.*
> —*John R. W. Stott[1]*

Will there be Jews, or Muslims, or Hindus in heaven? Few questions are as thorny, or as likely to highlight the differences between conservative and liberal Christians as this question. My aim here will not be to offer a comprehensive discussion of this question (I'll refer the reader to my book *Christianity and World Religions*[2] for a fuller treatment of the question). Instead I'll offer just a few words about the middle path between the two poles with regard to the answer to this question.

The conservative extreme or pole has a black-and-white answer to this question. The answer is "No"—there will be no persons in heaven who have not personally accepted Jesus Christ as their Lord and Savior. No Jews, no Hindus, no Muslims will be in heaven. This view is known as Christian exclusivism or particularism.

The most liberal pole, at least among those who believe in heaven, holds that all persons will ultimately be welcomed to heaven. This view is known as Christian universalism.

I am not comfortable with either of these answers. There are hundreds of millions of people who long to know God, who follow him according to what they know of his will, who pray daily to him—often putting most Christians to shame when it comes to their prayer life—and who earnestly seek to please God by doing what is just and right. We say that God forms such persons in their mothers' wombs, knows them by name, loves them, sees and hears every prayer they utter, and surely sees their attempts to do what is right as they understand it. Is

This image of these hundreds of millions who have earnestly sought God being tormented for eternity, whether God directly sends them to hell, or simply allows them to perish, seems neither loving, just, nor righteous.

it really the gospel truth that God then stands by and watches as they perish? Not only so, but must we believe as Christians that God has designed an eternal punishment—a torment—for them, because, though they sought God, they did not understand that Jesus is the Christ and they did not call upon him for salvation? This I find incomprehensible and completely out of character for a God whose defining characteristic, according to the Scriptures, is love, and whose secondary characteristics are justice and righteousness. This image of these hundreds of millions who have earnestly sought God being tormented for eternity, whether God directly sends them to hell, or simply allows them to perish, seems neither loving, just, nor righteous.

On the converse side, there are hundreds of millions of people who have, their entire lives, resisted God's will, who have not lived lives of love, who have not valued justice or mercy, and who lived lives in which they were the center of their existence. If heaven is a place where God's will is perfectly done, and where all yield to the divine will, where people naturally put others first, and where they always do what is right, such a place would be hell for all who resisted God and lived only for themselves. The only way they could enter heaven would be if God removed their freedom to choose or reject him. This I don't see God doing. And if God does not do this, and they enter heaven, heaven ceases to be heaven. I see two choices for such persons. Either their lives are snuffed out, as many believe will happen. They could have had eternal life, but instead they are eternally separated from God through a final death. Or they are allowed to go to a place where all of those souls who wish to live primarily for themselves, and who resist God and goodness go. Now, if you

If heaven is a place where God's will is perfectly done, and where all yield to the divine will, where people naturally put others first, and where they always do what is right, such a place would be hell for all who resisted God and lived only for themselves.

can imagine such a place, populated only by those who believe the world should revolve around them, and where all who sought to do right, and who brought sacrificial love into the world are not present, you have a picture of hell that begins to look Dantesque. (We'll develop this idea further in the next chapter: "The Logic of Hell.")

Those who hold a more conservative view on the fate of non-Christians are already thinking of a myriad of responses to my first statement. You're wondering, If people who sought God but did not understand or believe the gospel might be saved, then what is the source of their salvation? After all, we don't believe that people can be saved by their works. And you are remembering Jesus' words in John 14:6: "I am the way, and the truth, and the life. No one comes to the Father except through me," or some other similar passage. And perhaps you are wondering, If God allows those who have not received Jesus as their Lord and Savior into heaven, then why should we share the gospel with anyone at all? I'll address all of these questions in just a moment.

But first, allow me to point out that most liberals and conservatives already hold to some shade of gray on this issue.

Most liberals I know who believe that all will be saved will admit to at least a few exceptions—particularly those people who have done terrible and atrocious things and who seem to incarnate evil. Here we might think of murderous tyrants like Hitler.

Many of the conservatives I know would allow that God may judge nonbelievers, who have had no opportunity to receive Christ—the proverbial villagers on an island where no missionary has ever trod—according to how they responded to whatever "light" that they did have access to. Even those conservatives who reject this idea will often believe that children of believers who die before reaching the "age of accountability" will be granted God's mercy and will be welcomed to heaven. So some conservatives embrace a bit of gray on this issue as well.

Before exploring a third option between universalism and exclusivism, let's first consider the question of whether the Bible gives us any indication of how God may view those who are nonbelievers.

It is important to recognize that most of the Old Testament is devoted to telling the story of God's relationship to one particular people: the descendants of Israel. Yet the story doesn't begin with Israel, or even Abraham, but with the creation of humankind in Adam and Eve. And following the story of the flood, we find once more God's universal interest in humanity and God entering into a covenant with all of humanity (and even the animals). Following the flood, the rainbow was a sign of God's covenant with *all* humanity—a reminder, after the storm, of God's promise not to destroy the earth again by flood.

We see God's concern for other nations at various points in Israel's story. God promises Abraham that "all the nations of the earth shall be blessed [through you]" (Genesis 18:18). In Genesis 14 Abraham is blessed by Melchizedek, who is the king of Salem and priest of God Most High (this man, who is not a descendant of Abraham and apparently had no connection with Abraham prior to this event, becomes in the New Testament a predecessor or "type" of Jesus). God promises Hagar that he will make her son, Ishmael, into a great nation. Both Rahab (a Canaanite) and Ruth (a Moabite) are heroines in the Old Testament. Repeatedly in Isaiah God mentions his desire for the nations to come to him and his intention to offer light and salvation and peace to the nations.[3] Cyrus the Persian is actually called God's "messiah" ("anointed one") in Isaiah, and is the instrument of God to save his people and restore the exiles to the promised land (Isaiah 45:1). Isaiah clearly demonstrates God's universal concern for humanity.

Though the Old Testament is focused on the story of God's interaction with a particular people, haven't you wondered whether, over the course of the twelve hundred years from Abraham to Malachi, what God was doing in relationship to the other nations? Did God cease to look over them? Did he forget about the other children of the world? Or was he still watching over them the way he did over all the people from Noah to Abraham's time, whether they knew to call upon him or not?

It is interesting that in the ancient Near East, El, an abbreviated form of Elohim, was the "generic" name for "god," though it was also used to describe the chief of all the gods in the near eastern pantheon. Elohim is also the "generic" term for God in the Scriptures. Surely God heard and received the prayers and praise offered to him even if they were offered by people who had little knowledge of him.

Jonah is the most interesting among the books of the Bible in this regard. The underlying theological point is that God is concerned with the people in the Assyrian capital of Nineveh. He's even concerned with their animals. He has been watching them and their evil has reached a crescendo, and judgment will come upon them. But rather than simply destroy them, God wishes to call them to repentance and to show them mercy. These are people who worship a host of deities of the ancient Near East, including El.

Jonah is a prophet of God whom God calls to preach repentance to the Ninevites. He typifies the attitude of many in Israel who would rather see God destroy the Ninevites than show them mercy. Jonah is so opposed to this mission that he flees from God, and travels by ship in the opposite direction of Nineveh. In the end God is quite persuasive and Jonah submits to God's will. Jonah preaches to the Ninevites, calling them to repent; when they actually do so, God spares them. But Jonah is profoundly disappointed that God shows mercy to the Ninevites. God's closing

Would God not say the same thing today of India, China, Saudi Arabia, or his own land of Israel [as he said of Nineveh in the book of Jonah]? God is concerned about the nations.

words to Jonah are as follows: "Should I not be concerned about Nineveh, that great city, in which there are more than a hundred and twenty thousand persons who do not know their right hand from their left, and also many animals?" (Jonah 4:11).

Would God not say the same thing today of India, China, Saudi Arabia, or his own land of Israel? God is concerned about the nations. Again it is worth remembering that the Scriptures teach that God forms us in our mothers' wombs. I take that to mean that our unique character and certain innate gifts are from God, an idea confirmed by the psalm that tells us that we are fearfully and wonderfully made (Psalm 139:13-14). Surely this is true of all people, not just the Israelites and the Christians.

When we come to the New Testament we find that God's concern for the nations reaches its zenith in Jesus Christ, who brings salvation to all people. The very fact that Gentiles have been incorporated into the people of God is a sign of the depth of God's concern for those outside of his covenant people.

Matthew's gospel begins with this concern for the nations. It is not the shepherds who appear first on the scene to honor the Christ Child in Matthew. Instead it is magi from Persia (modern-day Iran) who come to pay homage to Jesus. They have "seen his star," a reminder that they are astrologers, and they are

God invited these men from some distance away to witness the birth of Jesus, and, interestingly enough, to bring gifts that would sustain the Christ child and his family on their flight to Egypt. What does this tell us about God?

likely followers if not priests of Zoroaster. I find this story interesting and insightful. God revealed the birth of Jesus to them in one of the ways they sought to hear from God—astrology—even though the Bible is generally opposed to astrology. And God invited these men from some distance away to witness the birth of Jesus, and, interestingly enough, to bring gifts that would sustain the Christ child and his family on their flight to Egypt. What does this tell us about God?

The Gospels have numerous references and hints of Jesus' concern for the nations, but it is in Acts, first with Peter and then with Paul, that we find God opens the floodgates so that non-Jews might come into his kingdom. Paul understands that in Christ, God has made it possible for Gentiles to be incorporated into the people of God even without being circumcised or obeying the Jewish law. Salvation is now a free gift made possible by the death of Christ. All that non-Jews must do to receive it is to have faith. And even this faith is a gift of the Holy Spirit.

There are a host of other clues in the New Testament regarding God's interest in those who are neither Jews nor Christians. Romans 1:20 seems to indicate that all human beings have access to some knowledge of God—a kind of general knowledge—and hence they are without excuse if they reject this knowledge of God. That would indicate that God judges some people based simply upon how they responded to this generic knowledge of God.

The closing verses of the Bible, in Revelation, give us a vision of the river of life flowing from the throne of God, with trees on either side, whose leaves are "for the healing of the nations" (Revelation 22:2). We are also told of the new Jerusalem that comes down out of heaven from God, that "the nations will walk by its light, and the kings of the earth will bring their splendor into it" (Revelation 21:24 NIV). Twenty-three times the phrase "kings of the earth" appears in the Bible, and in every case, including all other appearances of it in the book of Revelation, it refers to those who are nonbelievers. Generally, the term *nations* also means nonbelievers. This is why universalists will often point to this verse to demonstrate that the writer of Revelation seems to have in mind, in the end of this present world, that the nations will all be saved. Though I am less certain of this interpretation, I do think this verse indicates God's concern for the salvation of those outside of his own covenant people.

Finally, I would simply note that when we study Jesus, particularly in the Gospel of Luke, we find that his mission is to "seek out and to save the lost" (Luke 19:10). His stories about lost sheep and prodigal children point to the heart of God toward the lost. John tells us that God *is* love.

> When we study Jesus, particularly in the Gospel of Luke, we find that his mission is to "seek out and to save the lost" (Luke 19:10). His stories about lost sheep and prodigal children point to the heart of God toward the lost.

So, from a cursory reading of Scripture it would seem that God is concerned for all humankind, forms us all in our mothers' wombs, knows us each by name, and wishes for us to be saved.

If this is God's desire, then we must turn to a second question: How does the New Testament indicate that salvation for any of us is attained? Does it not teach that Christ's death was an atoning sacrifice for the sins of the world? Do we not learn, in that most famous of all gospel verses, that "God so loved *the world* that he gave his only son"? So, salvation is made possible by what Jesus has done for us. But how do we appropriate that salvation? We appropriate by believing in him—by faith. Paul writes in Ephesians: "By grace you have been saved through faith, and this is not your own doing; it is the gift of God—not the result of works, so that no one may boast" (Ephesians 2:8-9). So we do nothing to save ourselves; all we do is put our trust in God to save us. And even our capacity to trust is God's gift.

Now let's consider the plight of the *faithful* Hindu, Jew, or Muslim—and by faithful I mean the man or woman who is earnest in his or her faith, deeply desired God, and who seeks to live according to the demands of God as they understand those demands. Let's suppose this person has heard of Jesus. She has a generally positive view of Jesus (though, unfortunately, often her view of Jesus has been tainted by the reality of Christians who represent

> The likelihood [of a Hindu, Jew, or Muslim] actually converting is not much greater than the likelihood that you will respond to a Muslim missionary who would approach you.

him poorly). But the likelihood of her actually converting is not much greater than the likelihood that you will respond to a Muslim missionary who would approach you. It is possible, but not likely, that you would give her a fair hearing. So, in the case of the Hindu, Jew, or Muslim, she has heard a bit of the Christian gospel, remained unpersuaded yet positive about Jesus, and continues to trust in God and seeks to do God's will as she has been taught it by her parents and religious instructors. She bows, prays, studies, helps the poor, seeks to walk in humility, lives a life of service, and gives sacrificially. In her heart, she loves God, but is not persuaded, based upon the Christians she has met and heard from, that Christianity is the truth. Is there any hope for this person?

I believe that God, who is just and loving, sees this woman's heart. I also believe that it is by God's grace alone that she has sought God in her religion. I believe that God accepts what the person knows to bring, and that it is possible that she will be saved. All that she has brought to God is trust, which is all that any of us bring to God. And in response to her trust, she has sought to live according to God's precepts, as she understood them, which is what we have sought to do. I have several friends who are Muslims or Jews (I have not had the opportunity to develop long-term relationships with Hindus) who fulfill the great commandments better than many of the Christians that I know. Yes, I believe it is possible for God to save them.

"How can you make such a claim?" the exclusivist will ask. How can someone be saved by God if he has not personally accepted

Christ as his Lord and Savior? My answer is that I have, over the years, officiated at the funerals of more than a dozen children who were unable to truly accept Christ as their Savior. I've baptized children in the emergency room as they died, and prayed with families as we entrusted their little ones into God's care before removing life support. I would ask you, If you believe as I do that they are in heaven, how was their salvation possible? They were born into sin. How did God address the problem of their sinfulness in extending salvation to them?

The answer, I believe, is that God can apply the saving work of Jesus to anyone God chooses to apply it to. Christ's saving work was completed in the past. God appropriates or gives this gift of salvation. We know, in the New Testament, that the ordinary means of receiving that gift is simply by trusting in Christ as your Savior. But if you are unable to do that, as in the case of a child, it is possible for God to give that gift to you based on some other criteria. In the case of a child of a believer, we believe it is the love God has for children (Jesus said that we all must become like a child to enter the kingdom, and, in holding a child, he told his disciples, "The kingdom of God belongs to such as these") that leads God to give the gift of salvation to one who has not personally received it.

> God can apply the saving work of Jesus to anyone God chooses to apply it to.

In the same way, why would God not be able to give the gift of salvation, wrought by Jesus' suffering and death, to anyone that God chooses to give this gift to, based upon his mercy for someone who earnestly sought him, loved him, and responded to his mercy and grace in the only ways he knew to do so?

The exclusivist will object to this line of reasoning by citing certain scriptures: In John 3:18 Jesus says, "Those who believe in him are not condemned; but those who do not believe are condemned already, because they have not believed in the name of the only Son of God." In John 3:5 Jesus says, "Very truly, I tell you, no one can enter the kingdom of God without being born of water and Spirit." In John 14:6 Jesus says, "I am the way, and the truth, and the life. No one comes to the Father except through me." There are several other passages that are frequently cited as well.

Why would God not be able to give the gift of salvation, wrought by Jesus' suffering and death, to anyone that God chooses to give this gift to, based upon his mercy for someone who earnestly sought him, loved him, and responded to his mercy and grace in the only ways he knew to do so?

With regard to these scriptures I believe two things: First, when Jesus speaks, he almost always does so in what is sometimes called "prophetic hyperbole." That is, he exaggerates or makes broad statements to make a point. He tells us, "If your eye causes you to sin, pluck it out" (Mark 9:47 NIV). Yet we don't take this passage literally. We understand it means that sin is serious business and we should avoid it. He tells us that "unless you eat [my] flesh . . . and drink [my] blood, you have no life in you" (John 6:53-56 NIV). Catholics take this verse literally and it is a part of why they believe that in the Eucharist, rightly celebrated, the bread and wine become the body and blood of Christ. But most Protestants say, "Jesus is only using a figure of speech. This is not meant to be taken literally." He tells us "it is easier for a camel to go through the eye of a needle than for someone who is rich to enter the kingdom of God" (Matthew 19:24). But we don't read this passage literally. We understand that Jesus was offering a broad statement meant to make a point.[4] I would suggest that the same is true of these verses cited by the exclusivist.

In the case of Jesus' conversation with Nicodemus in John 3:5, it seems clear that Jesus wasn't trying to lay out for us a doctrine of the eternal destiny of those who don't know him. He was trying to tell Nicodemus that we are all in need of spiritual transformation. Neither in John 3:18 is Jesus trying to set forth a doctrine of the religions. He (or John) is trying to make a broad statement about rejecting the Son, and John notes that many will reject

Christ. These stand condemned. But even here it is worth asking, Does "standing condemned" necessarily mean sentenced to eternal damnation? Or is John simply noting that apart from the grace of Christ we all stand condemned of our sins? Such condemnation does not preclude God showing mercy upon the condemned. What about John 14:6, when Jesus states, "I am the way, and the truth, and the life. No one comes to the Father except through me"? Once again, I don't believe Jesus is attempting here to answer the question as to whether the faithful Hindu, Muslim, or Jew is going to spend eternity in hell. He is stating a fact—salvation is only through him. If God chooses to save anyone, including the Hindu, Muslim, or Jew, I believe it will only be by means of the saving work of Jesus—hence no Hindu, Muslim, or Jew would enter the kingdom of heaven except by the work of Christ, even if they did not know to call upon that work. In other words, no one comes to the Father but by him.

So, you might ask, why should we share the gospel with others, if they might be granted the gift of salvation apart from calling upon his name? Why have missionaries risked their lives to share the gospel in difficult places, even dying to share Christ?

Certainly many of them did so believing there was no hope for the people they were trying to reach apart from them hearing and responding to the gospel. But is our only motive for sharing Christ that we believe that the loving God we offer will eternally torment the souls of people in hell if they don't accept our offer of salvation? I spoke to a young man once who had turned away from Christianity in part over this question of whether non-Christians might be saved. Regarding the evangelistic messages of many conservatives, in which adherents of other religions were told that they would suffer in hell if they did not receive Christ, he said, "That's not loving. That's blackmail. That's coercion. There's something wrong with that picture." I think he's right.

Why do we share the gospel with others? Because we believe God will eternally torment all who did not accept Christ? Or because we believe the gospel is the truth about God and humankind? We share the gospel because we believe it is the hope of the world. We share the gospel with others because we believe the gospel is not just about heaven, but about having life even here on earth. We share the gospel because in it is a holistic salvation that brings to us unconditional love, mercy, and forgiveness; a new beginning; a new life; a mission for our lives; the body of Christ; and communion with God in a way not found in any other faith. And finally, we share Christ because he asked us to. Is this not enough?

This idea, that others might be saved by Christ's atoning work, even if they don't know or understand to call upon the name of Christ, is a middle position, usually called "inclusivism," that occupies the territory between universalism and exclusivism. It allows that some may reject the grace of God. It posits that Jesus' atoning work is the means by which God saves. And it maintains that salvation is not by works but by faith. It holds that in God's mercy, God will save many who sought him although they did not understand to call upon the name of Christ. This view seems, to me, to be more consistent with the justice, mercy, and love of God revealed in Jesus Christ than the exclusivist's view.

I am convinced that the God whose glory fills the cosmos, who calls each of the billions upon billions of stars by name, who sends his Son to reconcile and redeem the world, who is the Father in the story of the Prodigal Son, is not a small God. He must know that some of his children will not understand the gospel. They will have been raised by their parents as Hindus or Muslims or Jews and will find it far harder to accept the gospel than those of us raised by parents who were believers. Or they have had Christian witnesses who poorly represented Jesus. I do not believe he is a God who sends billions who love him and trust him, but did not understand the truth of the gospel, to eternity in hell.

> I am convinced that the God whose glory fills the cosmos, who calls each of the billions upon billions of stars by name, who sends his Son to reconcile and redeem the world, who is the Father in the story of the Prodigal Son, is not a small God.

I am reminded of the words of God to Samuel concerning King David: "The LORD does not see as mortals see; they look on the outward appearance, but the LORD looks on the heart" (1 Samuel 16:7b). And just as God applies the merits of Christ's atoning work to children and the mentally handicapped, and, some would say, to the faithful who lived before the time of Christ, so too, it seems to me, God can apply these merits to those who love God, seek God, and strive to serve God, but who either have never heard the gospel, or could not make sense of it.

I am reminded of the words of God to Samuel concerning King David: "The LORD does not see as mortals see; they look on the outward appearance, but the LORD looks on the heart" (1 Samuel 16:7b).

Before ending this chapter I thought, for the Evangelicals reading this book, that a few other witnesses to this idea of inclusivism might be helpful. In the early church Justin Martyr was said to have been an inclusivist. Ulrich Zwingli of the Reformers and, later, John Wesley, were inclusivists. C. S. Lewis held an inclusivist perspective, as was beautifully illustrated in the judgment scene in *The Last Battle* in his *Chronicles of Narnia*. And John R. W. Stott, the great evangelical Anglican evangelist writes, "I have never been able to conjure up (as some great Evangelical missionaries have) the appalling vision of the millions who are not only perishing but will inevitably perish. On the other hand . . . I am not and cannot be a universalist. Between these extremes I cherish and hope that the majority of the human race will be saved. And I have a solid biblical basis for this belief."[5]

Whether you are convinced by these arguments regarding inclusivism or not, Christians might learn a lesson from Billy Graham about humility regarding our willingness to make firm pronouncements that those of other religions are automatically excluded from heaven. In a recent cover story on Billy Graham in *Newsweek*, a story I have referred to earlier in this book, the author noted, "A unifying theme of Graham's new thinking is humility.

He is sure and certain of his faith in Jesus as the way to salvation. When asked whether he believes heaven will be closed to good Jews, Muslims, Buddhists, Hindus or secular people, though, Graham says: 'Those are decisions only the Lord will make. It would be foolish for me to speculate on who will be there and who won't . . . I don't want to speculate about all that. I believe the love of God is absolute. He said he gave his son for the whole world, and I think he loves everybody regardless of what label they have.' "[6]

In the end, what I believe about God and his judgment of those of other religions is captured in the words to a famous old hymn,

> There's a wideness in God's mercy like the wideness of the sea;
> there's a kindness in God's justice, which is more than liberty.

> There is welcome for the sinner, and more graces for the good;
> there is mercy with the Savior; there is healing in his blood.

> For the love of God is broader than the measure of our mind;
> and the heart of the Eternal is most wonderfully kind.[7]

Notes

1. David Edwards and John R. W. Stott, *Evangelical Essentials: A Liberal-Evangelical Dialogue* (Downers Grove, Ill.: InterVarsity, 1988), 327. This citation is quoted in a broader article on this subject, which includes numerous Scripture references, by Robin Brace at www.ukapologetics.net/evinc.htm.
2. Adam Hamilton, *Christianity and World Religions* (Nashville: Abingdon, 2005).
3. See Isaiah 2:2-4; 11:1-12; 12:1-3; 42:1-7; 49:6; 60:3; and others.
4. It is interesting that Roman Catholics take literally Jesus' words in John 6 about eating and drinking his flesh and blood through their doctrine of transubstantiation at the Eucharist—a doctrine that conservative Protestant Christians reject, though it is firmly based upon a literal reading of the words of Jesus.
5. Edwards and Stott, *Evangelical Essentials*, 327. Robin Brace quotes this citation in a broader article on this subject, which includes numerous Scripture references, www.ukapologetics.net/evinc.htm.
6. Jon Meacham, "Pilgrim's Progress," Newsweek, August 14, 2006, *Newsweek*, http://www.newsweek.com/id/46365.
7. Frederick William Faber, "There's a Wideness in God's Mercy," *The United Methodist Hymnal* (Nashville: The United Methodist Publishing House), 121.

Thirteen
The Logic of Hell

*I willingly believe that the damned are, in one sense, success-
ful, rebels to the end; that the doors of hell are locked on the inside.*
—C. S. Lewis

I suggested in the last chapter that there may be Hindus in heaven. This notion will likely be unsettling to many conservatives. I'd like to approach a notion in this chapter that might be unsettling to some liberals: the notion of hell and the reality that some people are destined to go there.

Hell seems, to many people, to be one of those doctrines that is inconsistent with the idea of a loving and merciful God. There are at least three dimensions of hell many find disturbing.

First, we are disturbed by the idea of good people being sent to hell. We can find the idea of hell more acceptable when we think of evil people who abuse, rape, and murder. But thinking of hell as a place where a loving grandfather, or a mother of small children, or a best friend might be sent simply because they did not understand or believe the gospel when it was presented to them is disturbing to many.

Second, we are disturbed by the idea of hell as torture and punishment for its inhabitants. We can relate to punishment—we've all been disciplined for doing wrong things. But as parents, when we discipline our children it is redemptive; that is, the intention is to teach them something and to shape their character. But even here we try to make sure that the punishment fits the crime. We would not torture our children for doing wrong. But the idea of the kind of punishment usually associated with hell—a torturous furnace of fire "where the worm dies not" (Mark 9:47-48, paraphrased), "where there will be weeping and gnashing of teeth" (Matthew 13:42)—is unsettling. Would the God whose nature is love create a place where people would be tortured by fire, or worse? Can we attribute to God the creation of a prison whose cruelty exceeds that of any prisons run by contemporary diabolical dictators?

Finally, the question is not simply who *populates* hell, nor the *kind* of torment that is experienced there, but the *duration* of the sentence to hell; namely, that hell is *eternal* punishment for those who have been sent there. Such a punishment is disproportionate to the crime—an eternity of suffering for eighty or ninety years of sin? Would God subject a soul to *eternal* torture for failing to respond to his offer of grace in this temporal life?

My aim in this chapter is not to offer a comprehensive statement about hell, but to describe a few ideas that shape my own view of hell—ideas that may either be helpful to you, or at least serve as a basis for clarifying your own view of hell. I reject the literalistic views of some conservatives concerning hell, and the dismissive and overly optimistic view of some liberals, but I would suggest a third set of possible views of hell and invite you to consider these in the light of Scripture, tradition, experience, and reason.

I reject the idea that there is no such place or state as hell. Jesus speaks with some regularity about judgment and a place of "outer darkness." He embodies this judgment when, in anger, he casts the moneychangers from the temple. I can picture his jaw clenched and the look in his eyes as he describes those dismissed from the Son of Man's presence at the Last Judgment for seeing the hungry, thirsty, and naked and doing nothing to help. I cannot ignore this idea of judgment if I am to take Jesus seriously.

> I reject the idea that there is no such place or state as hell. Jesus speaks with some regularity about judgment and a place of "outer darkness."

At the same time I recognize that Jesus speaks in metaphors and similes and uses hyperbole frequently in order to make his point. We must take Jesus' comments about the judgment and a negative afterlife seriously, but I don't believe we must take them literally, just as I don't think we take literally his command to cut off our hand or pluck out our eyes if they cause us to sin. These directives from Jesus are meant to be taken seriously, but not literally.

As an aside, I have heard a handful of people over the years describe near-death experiences that were not of the pleasant variety—near-death experiences that literally "scared the hell out" of them. One such man, an atheist before the experience, and now a United Church of Christ pastor, described his near-death experience this way:

"I always believed you died, and after that nothing—a kind of darkness—but now I was in that darkness, beyond life, and it was hell. . . . I was left alone to become a creature of the dark. . . . I desperately needed someone to love me, someone to know I was alive." He notes that at that moment the words and tune to a song he had learned when he was a small child began to enter his thoughts: "Jesus loves me, this I know." He continues that, as he began to sing this song, "for the first time in my adult life I wanted it to be true that Jesus loved me. I didn't know how to express what I wanted and needed, but with every bit of my last ounce of strength I yelled out into the darkness 'Jesus save me' . . . far off in the distance, I saw a pinpoint of light." [1] Shortly after this the doctors resuscitated him. His experience of a place of utter darkness seems consistent with some of the biblical descriptions of hell.

I want to return to say a word to those reading who may be a bit more conservative, and who believe that there are many who are going to hell. I would encourage you to take the time to study what Jesus says about who is going to hell. Those who are going to hell, according to Jesus, are those who call their neighbor a "fool" (Matthew 5:22b); those who lust after women in their hearts (Matthew 5:27-30); religious leaders who are hypocritical (Matthew 23:1-36); those who are not good stewards of the gifts God has given them (Matthew 25:14-30); and religious people who refuse to help those in need (Matthew 25:31-46). Nothing is said in these passages about people of other religions, or even lost people; most of what Jesus says about hell seems reserved for those who are religious. Most of us have said to another "You fool!" Most of us have lusted after others in our hearts. We've all acted with hypocrisy. And none of us have done as much as we should have done to help those in need.

I think Jesus uses hell as a way of warning us to take our sin seriously, just as I warn my teenage daughters that they will be grounded for the "rest of your lives" if they lie to me, or they will lose their right to drive for "months" if I catch them driving without their seatbelt, or I will refuse to pay for a cent of their college if they get any kind of extraneous piercing or tattoo while they are still on my "payroll." I mean for them to take me very seriously when I say these things, but ultimately my mercy prevails and the judgment, though meted out, is typically of a briefer duration than the threat. The threat is like saying, "This is the maximum penalty by law," but I reserve the right to lower the penalty.

Yet I believe in hell. I do so not simply because Jesus talked about it but because it seems to me to be a necessary and logical corollary to heaven. Jesus tells us that we are to pray "thy kingdom come, thy will be done, on earth as it is in heaven." This tells us something about heaven—it tells us that in heaven God's will is done. If heaven is that place where God's reign is complete, where God's will is always done, where people no longer hate, kill, steal, mistreat, go to war, or inflict pain on others, then those who enter must either have their freedom removed, or they agree to submit to God's reign and will.

But what if someone is unwilling to live according to God's will? Would that person be forced to dwell in the heavenly kingdom? I don't think so. Such an existence would be a hell for them, and heaven would no longer be a place where God's will is done. Hell, it seems to me, is the place for all of those who do not wish

> Yet I believe in hell. I do so not simply because Jesus talked about it but because it seems to me to be a necessary and logical corollary to heaven.

> Hell, it seems to me, is the place for all of those who do not wish to live according to God's will and submit their lives to God's reign.

to live according to God's will and submit their lives to God's reign. God wishes all to join him and to live as his children and his subjects. He is a good King, a benevolent King, and a loving King. But he will not force persons to be his subjects. He beckons them to choose, and to willingly follow him. If one does not wish to do this, there is a place, a kind of dark kingdom, reserved for all who wish to do things their own way.

Let's consider what this hell must be like. If it is populated by those who wish not to live according to the will of God, then it is filled with those who wish to do things their own way. It is filled with people who believe the world revolves around them. It is filled with people who are always "looking out for number one"; countless narcissistic souls who are taking advantage of other narcissistic souls in order to meet their own needs—people feeding on one another until there is nothing left to feed on. Hell would be a place where most goodness has been removed, where the restraints that come from people following God have been removed, and where the light of God's presence may be dim, or absent altogether.[2] Dante may not have been far off in describing one scene from hell where one resident is gnawing on the flesh of another. In essence,

> It is filled with people who believe the world revolves around them. It is filled with people who are always "looking out for number one"; countless narcissistic souls who are taking advantage of other narcissistic souls in order to meet their own needs—people feeding on one another until there is nothing left to feed on.

this may be a powerful picture of hell—a place filled with the self-absorbed, absent of nearly all goodness, darkened as we would expect by the desire to be as far away from God's reign as possible.

What's important to note in this concept is that hell is a nightmare, and the nightmare is not the result of something God has created, but the result of the exercise of freedom on the part of inhabitants who have chosen to reject God's rule and reign.

Not long ago a woman who had escaped the Congo shared her story with the staff of our church. The horrors she described in her country gave me a picture of what hell must be like. She spoke of homes destroyed, property confiscated, brutal murders, cannibalism, and of her own rape and the rape of her children. She showed photos so gruesome that, after I wrote a description of them here I decided to take it out—it is simply too disturbing. These events are happening now, today, by men who are utterly depraved and who have the ability to do whatever they wish wherever they wish. Do we really believe such men would submit to the rule of God and enter the kingdom of heaven? This is my picture of the inhabitants of hell ever seeking to do whatever they wish to one another. This is utter darkness where there is weeping and gnashing of teeth.

I have one last thought about hell, and perhaps heaven, for that matter. Is it possible that those in heaven might choose to rebel against God's rule at some time in the future? Many Christian theologians suggest that once we are in heaven, we find it impossible to sin. Perhaps, but is it possible, even in heaven, that we might rebel, and that God might let us go to the place reserved for those who rebel against him? And, likewise, I wonder if it is possible that some in hell could choose to leave hell and yield or submit to God's will?

What if hell itself is aimed at working out God's redemptive purposes? What if the aim of hell is not only punishment or discipline, nor even simply God's provision of a place for those who wish to live outside of his will? What if God's hope is that those in hell will finally come to understand

What if hell itself is aimed at working out God's redemptive purposes?

the darkness of living for self and in rebellion to God, so that they will cry out, even from hell, "Lord Jesus, be merciful to me a sinner"?[3]

C. S. Lewis seems to suggest this view in his wonderful little book *The Great Divorce*. In it he notes that the doors of hell are "locked from the inside." The story tells of a busload of people in hell who journey to heaven and are given the opportunity to yield and stay in heaven, but one by one they choose to return to hell rather than live in the light of God's will. Lewis notes, "There are only two kinds of people in the end: those who say to God, 'Thy will be done,' and those to whom God says, in the end, 'Thy will be done.'"[4]

May we be those who say to him, daily, "Thy will be done."

Notes

1. Howard Storm, *My Descent into Death* (New York: Doubleday, 2005), 9, 24-25.
2. I am hesitant to think that God's presence is not in hell at all for the same reason that Psalm 139 suggests that even in Sheol (the place of the dead) God is there. I am uncertain whether there could be any place where God is not present.
3. The parable of Dives and Lazarus would indicate that those in hell could not repent and cross over, but that story is only a parable and is meant to teach a different point. The question, nevertheless, remains only in the realm of speculation.
4. C. S. Lewis, *The Great Divorce* (New York: Macmillan, 1946), 69.

Fourteen
Where Is God When Bad Things Happen?

How long, LORD? Will you forget me forever?
How long will you hide your face from me?

How long must I wrestle with my thoughts
and day after day have sorrow in my heart? . . .

But I trust in your unfailing love;
my heart rejoices in your salvation.
—Psalm 13:1–2, 5a TNIV

Among the most important and persistent questions we ask as human beings is the question of suffering. Why do bad things happen to good people? When you are a Christian, and you assert that you believe in a good and loving God, the problem of suffering becomes even more pronounced. Put succinctly, the question is: "If God is good and loving, and all-powerful, why doesn't God put a stop to suffering?"

As a pastor I have walked with hundreds of families through terrible crises, and I have had to wrestle with this question for these families, and for myself. The answer to the question theologians call "theodicy"—the problem of reconciling the goodness of God with the evil that happens in our world—is one that entire volumes have been devoted to addressing. My intention in this chapter is not to completely solve this problem (I cannot completely resolve every dimension of it myself) but to help you think critically about two of the most common answers given to the problem of

121

suffering, and to offer a third alternative—an answer that has helped me make sense of the interplay between God and suffering.

Let's begin by defining two common approaches to the problem of suffering.

The first is Deism. Deism is a view of God held by many of our nation's Founding Fathers. It holds that God created the universe and set in motion the laws that govern its operation, but beyond this initial work, God is not directly involved in the workings of our universe. God does not intervene in our affairs. The universe is a closed system. Suffering happens as a result of the human violation of the laws God established, and as a result of the natural processes that make our planet work—storms, earthquakes, and so forth. God neither causes suffering, nor does he intervene to stop it.

The second approach to the problem of God and suffering is what is known as Theological Determinism.[1] According to this view God is not only involved in our world, God has predetermined everything that will happen on earth. God is sovereign; he controls all things, knows all things; and is all-powerful. God has a plan and everything that happens does so according to his plan. He has written a script, and we are merely actors in God's play. Since God is ultimately good, loving, and just, we can trust that everything that happens will ultimately result in good; if things do not seem to be working out now, it is simply because we do not perceive all of God's plan at this moment. This view is commonly accepted without question by many Christians, and it is often expressed by the phrases "Everything happens for a reason," or, in resignation in the face of suffering, "It must be God's will."

> I consider both Deism and determinism to be inadequate, and ultimately unhelpful, approaches to the problem of evil.

I consider both Deism and determinism to be inadequate, and ultimately unhelpful, approaches to the problem of evil. I'll begin by offering a few objections before proposing a third way.

The challenge with Deism is that it undermines the entire premise of the Bible. The Bible presupposes, throughout its pages, that God *is* involved in our world. God knows us by name. God shapes us in our mothers' wombs. God chooses Israel as his covenant people, leads them out of slavery in Egypt, hears and answers the prayers of his people, and is at work in Israel's story as it unfolds. More than that, the Christian gospel proclaims that God is so involved in our world that he became flesh and walked among us, teaching, guiding, healing, and ultimately suffering and dying to redeem and save the world. Christianity teaches that God's Spirit dwells in us and comforts, guides, and empowers us. I find elements of Deism helpful, but when its premise is fully fleshed out, it stands in contrast to much of the biblical story.

While the objection to Deism might be covered in a paragraph, I would like to devote significantly more time to the objections to determinism, in large part because this view dominates the thinking of so many Christians today, and I believe it needs to be seriously questioned.

Let me begin with the implications of Christian determinism. If everything happens for a reason, this implies that God is, in fact, directing everything to happen. God not only knows it will happen, everything happens because God has a reason for it to happen. Though God is not the direct agent acting to bring about a certain action, because God planned it, he is the ultimate cause of the event. I want to invite you to consider this carefully.

An eight-year-old girl was brutally raped by two adults. The torture she endured left her body so damaged that it would require multiple surgeries to repair. Emotionally, it will take years of therapy for her and her entire family to begin to heal. When I first read of her story in the newspaper I could feel nothing but rage toward those who had committed this crime. The two who committed this crime also raped and murdered two women on their killing spree. According to the determinist: God predetermined that this would happen. God wrote it into the script. Yes, there were two human agents who actually committed the crime, but they committed the crime because God had predetermined that they would. Does this sound like the plans or purposes of a loving and just God?

Presumably, God predestined that these rapists and murderers would do what they did for some greater good that God has planned, and that we cannot see. But can there be any greater good that would justify brutalizing a little girl, and torturing and killing two women? If we learned that some person had hatched this plot and put these two murderers up to this, that person would be imprisoned. If God is just and good and loving, then the means he uses to accomplish his plans will also be just and good and loving.

> I have been in the midst of too many terrible tragedies, and too many experiences of evil, to attribute these things in any ultimate sense to God. No, I don't believe everything happens for a reason.

I have been in the midst of too many terrible tragedies, and too many experiences of evil, to attribute these things in any ultimate sense to God. No, I don't believe everything happens for a reason if, by this, someone means that the evil happened according to the will of God. In fact, what happened to that little girl, and most of the evil that I see happening in the world, is in every way antithetical to the nature and character of God. I consider it blasphemy of the worst kind to attribute such evil to God.

When Jesus walked this earth, he loved children and revealed God's heart to us concerning children. This God *does not* plan for such evil to be done to children.

If, when we say, "everything happens for a reason," we mean that the world is based upon cause and effect, I can accept this. The cause behind a friend's cancer is a problematic piece of DNA that led to the reproduction of millions (or billions?) of cells that continued to multiply, wreaking havoc on his body. The cause of the little girls' torment that I have described was a very sick man and woman who were very broken. These are the "reasons" behind what happened. But if by saying "everything happens for a reason," we

> I consider it blasphemy of the worst kind to attribute such evil to God.

mean that God wills everything, I can only pray that God is not truly like this.

I was once a determinist. This changed twenty-five years ago. I was a freshman in college, and newly married. It was seven o'clock one evening when I received a phone call at work. The person on the other end of the phone told me that Gary and Danny had died that afternoon in a terrible accident. Gary was my youth pastor who had helped me come to faith in Christ and mentored me in my faith. Danny was his little brother, and the best man in my wedding. He was, after my wife, my best friend.

Gary and Danny had been working for a roofing company. Their job was to deliver bundles of shingles to job sites where new roofs were being put on homes. The shingles were loaded onto a large boom truck—a flatbed truck with a hydraulic conveyor that was raised and moved to the rooftop, and then activated to convey the shingles to the roof. Danny was moving the hydraulic boom to the roof of a house, and he did not see the power lines overhead. When the boom hit the power lines, he was killed instantly, and his body was thrown from the truck. Gary saw this happen and ran to try to save his brother, by beginning CPR. He then looked up and saw that there were three other guys on the roofing crew who were "stuck" to the truck by the electrical current. Gary left Danny, grabbed a two-by-four, and pried the guys from the truck. When he did, the current from their bodies entered his body, and he was killed. The three roofers survived.[2]

My wife, LaVon, and I drove back to Kansas City from Tulsa to attend the visitation. I listened to various people as they tried to make sense of this. I overheard one person say, "I think Danny had sin in his life, and this was God's judgment on him." I had to walk away from that conversation or I was going to hurt the man who said this. Later I heard another person say, "God loved Gary and Danny so much he wanted them in heaven." I wondered, Is that how it works? If God really loves you he causes your early death? That didn't make much sense either. At the funeral another man suggested that Gary and Danny died so that someone at the funeral would give his or her life to Christ. I was certain that Gary and Danny would have loved for someone to have come to faith in Christ at their funeral, but I wondered, Is that really how God works? Did he bring about the death of my friends just to lead someone to Christ at their funeral service? It did not seem a very effective form of evangelism, and wouldn't my friends have led far more people to faith across the course of their lives had they lived?

I wrestled with these questions for months. I so firmly believed that "everything happens for a reason" and that God was in control of everything. The implication of this was that Gary's and Danny's deaths were the will of God. But I could not make sense of this. And my struggle was intensified by the fact that I was studying to be a pastor—to represent this God who had taken my friends' lives. I wasn't sure I could do it. At one point I felt I was losing my mind, or at least my faith.

My mother-in-law, Bernice, an active member of The United Methodist Church, played a catalytic role in helping me resolve this crisis of faith through something she said as I sat in her house, in tears, following the visitation—though it took me months to fully process it. I was asking the question "Why?" Bernice came and put her arm around me and said, "Adam, sometimes things like this just happen. There is no reason. Accidents like this happen sometimes." This sounds so simple, but up to this point I had no place in my thinking for accidents.

> Bernice came and put her arm around me and said, "Adam, sometimes things like this just happen. There is no reason. Accidents happen."

This is what I eventually came to understand as the answer to the question Why did Gary and Danny die? Danny died because he was operating a hydraulic boom and didn't notice the power lines, and when he struck the power line, the current that came into his body was enough to kill a human being. And Gary died because, when he saw that there were three people who were facing death, he thought more of them than he thought of himself, and he pried them free, and the laws of physics are such that the current that was in their bodies, when transferred to his body, was sufficient to kill a human being. This is why Gary and Danny died.

So where is God in all of this? God created the world along with laws that govern it. God created us with a capacity to reason, to make choices, including the choice to risk and sacrifice ourselves to save others. God allows us to live and to do things that are at times dangerous, like drive cars and operate heavy equipment.

But where else was God in all of this? Both Gary and Danny claimed Jesus as their Savior. But this did not mean that Jesus would save them from ever getting hurt. How could we think this is the promise of a faith whose central figure was crucified? Jesus promised to never let them go. He promised to "prepare a place for [them]" and he promised "I am the resurrection and the life. Those who believe in me . . . will never die." He promised "When this life is over, you have a building, not made by human hands, eternal in the heavens" (John 14:2; John 11:25-26; and 2 Corinthians 5:1, paraphrased). God was holding Gary and Danny in his arms.

God was also working to comfort and care for Gary and Danny's family and friends by his Spirit, the Comforter. The knowledge that Gary and Danny were with Christ gave the family and friends hope in the midst of their grief. God also promised that he would force good to come from this tragedy (Romans 8:28). God doesn't kill people in order to bring about this good, but he promises, in the face of tragedy, to use it for good. No suffering or tragedy is ever wasted by God. In so many ways God brought good from this and used this tragedy for his redemptive purposes. I am just one example of this. The deaths of Danny and Gary profoundly changed me; their lives and their deaths altered the course my life took, and the kind of pastor I am. I do not believe God "took them" so that I could be changed. But through their deaths God worked in the hearts and lives of many people, including me.

I am suggesting that we are not pawns on a chessboard, simply moved here and there by God. I am suggesting that we are not

We are not pawns on a chessboard, simply moved here and there by God. merely characters in God's tragic play. I am suggesting that God is not like the pathetic wizard in *The Wizard of Oz*, standing behind a curtain pushing buttons and pulling levers to cause us to, at every moment, take this turn or that. Instead, God has given us a universe with certain rules—rules we can discover and count on. He has given us the freedom to make decisions, to take risks, to do things that are exciting and dangerous. He has given us the potential to do good, but God himself also takes a great risk by giving us the potential to do harm. God allows us to build our homes in floodplains and hurricane-prone areas. God lets us smoke cigarettes, overeat, or become addicted to alcohol. And God will allow us to abuse our freedom, to hurt and even kill one another.

It is for this reason that God has, at times, grieved that he ever created us.[3] And yet God has a way of bringing about his redemptive purposes through the tragic things that happen on our planet, and the terrible things we sometimes do to one another. The cross of Christ is the prime example of this. Human beings crucified Jesus. They abused him, humiliated him, and then killed him. Evil seemed to triumph. But God used this human evil as an instrument of reconciliation, atonement, and salvation for the world.

Can God intervene in the world directly, stopping accidents from happening, protecting us from the harm others would do to us, averting natural disasters, and miraculously healing our diseases? Yes. God can do anything God wishes to do. But God's ordinary way of working in our world is less direct than that. God's ordinary way of working is to guide us by the Scriptures, the church, and the Spirit's witness, **God's ordinary way of working is to guide us by the Scriptures, the church, and the Spirit's witness, and to use doctors and medicine and others who seek to do what is right in order to help us and sustain us.**

and to use doctors and medicine and others who seek to do what is right in order to help us and sustain us. God's ordinary way is not to intervene directly, even though a million times a day God must grieve over the terrible things that humanity does.

Suffering does not occur because our faith is weak, but through it our faith may be strengthened.

And God's ordinary way is to clean up after us, and to use the pain and tragedy in our lives, to accomplish his purposes.

My friend Ray, who passed away a few years ago, once shared with me something he had found helpful in making sense of God and suffering. Ray was a pastor. His wife had been killed in a tragic railroad accident when her car was hit by an oncoming train. She left behind three small children for Ray to raise while working through his own grief. Ray never believed that God caused this accident. He knew that accidents happen. Years ago he gave me a clipping from a newsletter—a clipping he had found helpful—that read:

> Suffering is not God's desire for us, but it occurs in the process of life. Suffering is not given to teach us something, but through it we may learn. Suffering is not given to punish us, but sometimes it is the consequence of our sin or poor judgment. Suffering does not occur because our faith is weak, but through it our faith may be strengthened. God does not depend on human suffering to achieve his purposes, but sometimes through suffering his purposes are achieved. Suffering can either destroy us, or it can add meaning to our life.[4]

Does this statement capture the entirety of God's providential work in our lives? Perhaps not. I can think of exceptions to it. But it offers a corrective to the idea that everything that happens, happens for a reason, and that suffering, tragedy, and evil are God's will.

This leads me to a couple of final points. I wonder if God's perspective on our lives and deaths is different from our own. God has been overseeing creation for 14 billion years, and our planet for 4 billion years. Our lifespan, whether we live 5 years or 100 years,

Yet from God's eternal perspective, all of our suffering, and even our death, is but a "slight momentary affliction [that] is preparing us for an eternal weight of glory beyond all measure."

is microscopic compared to eternity. We are specks of dust, and yet God knows us by name. Every minute 106 people die—more than 2,000 have died as you read this chapter, and today 152,000 people will pass away. And God sees each one, knows the circumstances of their deaths, and often grieves at the loss we experience and the form these deaths often take. Yet from God's eternal perspective, all of our suffering, and even our death, is but a "slight momentary affliction [that] is preparing us for an eternal weight of glory beyond all measure" (2 Corinthians 4:17).

God comforts those who mourn, walks with us through the valley of the shadow of death, and redeems the suffering that happens in this world, forcing it to serve his purposes. He calls his people to work toward alleviating suffering and to act as instruments of healing in this world. But God has also given us the one antidote to death: the promise of the resurrection. He not only gave us a verbal promise of the resurrection, he came and walked among us, was himself subjected to the evil that we experience, suffered, and died, and then rose again in order to demonstrate that death is not the end. This is God's solution to the suffering and evil and tragedy in this world.

Early in my ministry I received a phone call from a nearby hospital asking that I come quickly–there had been a tragic accident and a family needed me. When I arrived in the emergency room I found a young couple, holding their three-year-old son, surrounded by doctors and nurses. Their son had been struck by a car and had just died. His parents asked if I could baptize him and, with a basin of water quickly prepared by the emergency room nurses, I took him in my arms and baptized him, committing him to God's love and care.[5]

That was more than a dozen years ago. I recently asked his parents if they had any words they could offer that would help me minister to another family who had just lost a child. I thought you might find their words meaningful:

The little boy's father said: "My faith grew, but not at first. I believe the despair and darkness of not having faith made me realize that the only way to go on without hatred and anger consuming my life was to embrace God and the idea of heaven. For me, faith doesn't fix problems, but it helps you to cope and survive, and eventually grow through the inevitable tragedies that everyone will have to face."

His wife had this to say: "I had had people tell me that it was [my son's] 'time,' and I was having a hard time believing in a God who would plan to take my child at age three. I learned that tragedies weren't necessarily part of God's plan, but that God gave us free will, and sometimes bad things happen. Understanding this helped me to turn to God instead of away from him. . . . Since [my son's] death, I believe that my faith has grown and continues to grow. His death changed the way I view God and my faith. I no longer have a naive, childlike faith where God protects you from all harm and makes everything OK. It's a deeper faith that has been tested through tragedy. I know that God doesn't promise me a pain-free life, but he does promise to always be there to love me, comfort me, and guide me. My faith gives me something that people without faith don't have—*hope*, hope for the future and the knowledge that I will see [my son] again in heaven."

Between the picture of a God who is not involved in our lives and world, and a God who causes everything to happen, is a picture of God who grants human beings freedom and the ability to risk; a God who does not cause tragedy but who uses it and brings good from it; a picture of a God who can directly and supernaturally intervene, but who usually works indirectly through people; and a picture of a God who ultimately heals us, and assures us that, in the end, "death has been swallowed up in victory" (1 Corinthians 15:54).

Notes

1. While this view often goes by this name, what I am describing is specifically Christian theism—a view that is closely associated with Calvinism, particularly in its strictest interpretations.

2. I have never spoken to the roofers Gary saved, but this is how the story was passed on to me twenty-five years ago.
3. This is the central point of the Noah story in Genesis 6. It appears clear there that God decides to put an end to humanity because God is grieved by the violence human beings are inflicting upon one another. This story is one of many that seem to undermine the idea of determinism.
4. This quotation comes from an unidentified church newsletter.
5. I believed that the child was with God already, and his baptism was not necessary for his salvation, but that it was important for his parents and all in that room to have this outward and visible sign of God's grace and love for this little boy.

Fifteen
In Praise of Honest Doubt

There lives more faith in honest doubt, believe me, than in half the creeds.
—Alfred, Lord Tennyson

Only God and certain madmen have no doubts!
—Martin Luther

Doubt is a universal human experience. Regardless of your faith, or lack of faith, certainty is hard to come by. This is true not only in matters of religion but also in life. Before marrying my wife, LaVon, I was 90 percent sure our marriage was God's will and that it would work out—but there was at least 10 percent doubt. I'm pretty sure I'm going to live a long life and be here to provide for my family. But I have life insurance just in case. And every time I get on an airplane, I feel confident that I'll make it to where I'm going and back home again, but I always leave a note to my wife and kids telling them I love them, in the event I don't return home. There are few certainties in life.

When it comes to matters of religion—questions of whether there is a God or not—we can expect a measure of uncertainty. This is true for the atheist and for the believer. I am reminded of one atheist (who later became a Christian) who told of the anxiety he experienced as an unbeliever when he considered the possibility that God

> We are all going to have periods of doubt when our faith seems ridiculous and we have more questions than answers.

might actually exist. What is true for the atheist is certainly going to be true for the Christian. We are all going to have periods of doubt when our faith seems ridiculous and we have more questions than answers.

Some fear doubt. They fear that doubt might be just the tip of the iceberg, and that if they allow themselves to doubt, they might very well fall away from God. Others believe doubt must surely displease God, and so, for God's sake, they can't allow themselves to admit to doubt.

I don't see doubt this way. Doubt is not only natural, it is healthy, provided it spurs us to further reflection and a search for what is true. Most of us wrestle with doubt from time to time, and our doubts become particularly pronounced in the face of adversity, or when encountering persons who see the world differently than we do. Some periods of time in our lives leave us searching, questioning, and wrestling with doubt. The late teen and early college years are commonly a time of doubt and searching for many. These doubts and questions may lead to a crisis point, a place where all we thought we knew for certain has been called into question, and our religious, philosophical, and moral foundations are shaken.

> Doubt is not only natural, it is healthy, provided it spurs us to further reflection and a search for what is true.

These crises commonly produce one of three responses: Some come to reject everything they had learned growing up, and the faith that they were raised with, and instead they turn away from God altogether. Others suppress their questions, and retreat to an intractable faith—a faith that is filled with certainties and is immune to questions. Often this is a fundamentalism that offers certainties, an inerrant Bible, and lots of reassurance that what one believes is absolutely true. But there is a third option, one that faces doubt head-on, and that carefully examines the presuppositions and assumptions of the faith that we've held up to this point. It accepts that there may well be truth in the faith we were raised with, while recognizing that not all we were taught may be true.

Parents are often unsettled when their children enter this phase of questioning. They can take it quite personally. They also fear that their own children may turn away from God and never find their way back. I have known this experience. My oldest daughter came to a point of questioning and even rejecting her faith for a time in her teen years. She announced to her youth camp counselors one summer: "I'm not a Christian." This generated quite a response from the counselors: the senior pastor's daughter was not a Christian. At the time I had a range of feelings. I felt like a failure. How could I preach the gospel to the church, while my own daughter had rejected it? I also felt rejection; I felt she was turning away from everything I stand for and believe in.

With my mind I knew that her struggle with faith was a good thing, that she needed to discover her own faith and that the doubts and the faith struggles would ultimately lead her to a faith that was richer and deeper than one she simply accepted without question from her mother and father. But in my heart, I felt afraid. I was afraid that she might turn away and never come back, and that this would lead her down a path in life that would be painful and difficult, or simply one where she did not have the hope of the gospel. I kept reminding myself of Proverbs 22:6: "Train children in the right way, and when old, they will not stray." The verse doesn't promise that when they are teens they won't stray, but when they are *old* they will not depart from the faith.

135

At night, after Danielle was asleep, I would slip into her bedroom, kneel next to her bed, and pray for her, that God would not let her go, and that he would keep her from harm. I prayed that God would give me wisdom and patience, and that he would reveal himself to her in ways that she could see and understand. In the end, she reclaimed her Christian faith, but now it was her own faith, not simply something her mother and father had taught her.

Os Guinness once wrote, "If ours is an examined faith, we should be unafraid to doubt. If doubt is eventually justified, we were believing what clearly was not worth believing. But if doubt is answered, our faith grows stronger still. It knows God more certainly and it can enjoy God more deeply." [1]

> "If ours is an examined faith, we should be unafraid to doubt. If doubt is eventually justified, we were believing what clearly was not worth believing. But if doubt is answered, our faith has grown stronger. It knows God more certainly and it can enjoy God more deeply."
>
> —Os Guinness

The Bible is filled with stories of people who had their doubts about whether God was there, or if God had actually called them to do what they had been told, or that God would be with them. Abraham, Moses, Gideon, and David all knew these doubts. So did Peter and John, even after seeing the empty tomb! And Thomas, though he had heard from his friends that they had all seen Jesus raised, refused to believe until he touched Jesus with his own hands.

If you are willing to take seriously the challenges and questions that arise from an examined faith, you will find yourself wrestling with doubt from time to time. How grateful I am for the prayer of the father of Mark 9, whose son is plagued with seizures. The man says to Jesus, "If you can do anything, take pity on us and help us." Jesus replies, " 'If you can'? . . . Everything is possible for [the one] who believes." And the boy's father exclaims, "I do believe; help me overcome my unbelief!" (vv. 23-24 NIV).

This has been my prayer on many occasions as well. "Lord, I believe; help my unbelief."

There is one last word about doubt that I think is important. It is possible to be paralyzed by doubt and uncertainty. This is not God's will for our lives. We are to face our doubts and allow them to lead us to a greater search for answers and a more examined faith. But sometimes we get stuck in doubt and we never act. If I hung onto my doubt, and allowed it to paralyze me, I would never have married. I would never have had children. I would never have taken my first airplane ride. I would have never jumped off of the high dive when I was eight. I would never have moved away to college. I would never have become a pastor.

At some point you look at the evidence you have, you weigh the testimony of others, including the witness of the Bible itself, you consider your own personal experiences, you weigh your options, and you make a decision to trust. And sometimes the only prayer you have is, "Lord, I believe; help my unbelief."

Note

1. Os Guinness, *God in the Dark: The Assurance of Faith Beyond a Shadow of a Doubt* (Wheaton, Ill.: Crossway Books, 1996), 14-15.

Sixteen
The Messy Truth about Spirituality

*If I were to die today, I would be nervous what people would
say at my funeral. I would be happy if they said things like, "He
was a nice guy" or "He was occasionally decent" or "Mike wasn't
as bad as a lot of people." Unfortunately eulogies are delivered by
people who know the deceased and the consensus would be, "Mike
was a mess."*
—Mike Yaconelli [1]

Do you ever feel like you don't quite get it? About the spiritual
life, I mean. You want to get it. You want to be a truly spiritual person. You're trying. But you don't feel the "joy unspeakable
and full of glory" that your fellow Christians seem to have. You
still struggle with temptation. You don't "pray without ceasing."
Your faith can't move dust bunnies, much less mountains. You only
have glimpses of the "peace that passes all understanding."

You feel you must be in the remedial group. Yet you're too
afraid to admit this to anyone, because you're certain they're getting it, and you'll just be embarrassed.

Somehow we think that maybe we can find the key to real
spirituality in a book. We go on a quest for the secret *gnosis*—
the knowledge we need to finally experience the Christian life
we've always wanted. We read Nouwen, or Merton, or Foster, or
Willard, or Tozer, or whomever it is that your particular branch
of Christianity views as an expert in the spiritual life. You read
this book and then that one, and sometimes it helps—you feel
inspired and encouraged, for a little while. Sometimes not. And
then, once more, you find yourself feeling like the same old remedial Christian.

I think one of the reasons I love that classic U2 hit "I Still Haven't Found What I'm Looking For" is because it captures that restless spirit most of us have—that sense that we still haven't quite got "it" yet.

So, who can help us find what we're looking for? We turn to our pastors, and they teach us the spiritual disciplines, and how to read the Bible, and they offer us words from the Scriptures for our daily lives. But this doesn't seem to be enough. We need something more. Some of us begin to think that the problem may not be that we're remedial—perhaps we're too advanced for the stuff our pastor and the books are offering us. Where can we go to find some real "meat" that will help us take the next step?

Recently I heard Bill Hybels, pastor of Willow Creek Community Church, describing how some in his church had noted that they didn't feel they were being "fed" and that they were wanting more. His reaction was one every pastor can relate to. He was at first defensive and disappointed, and he took the comments personally, as though it was a sign that he was failing as a pastor. He announced to his staff, "I'm not feeding them? I'll show them. I'll hire some old seminary professor and I'll have him feed them till they barf!" What Bill and his team concluded, however, is something we've been telling people in our church for years. Our job, as a church, is not to spoon-feed people the "deep truths of the faith" for their entire lives. Our job is to equip them with the basic tools and resources so that they can spend the rest of their lives daily pursuing their relationship with Christ and faithfully serving him in the world. Hybels described it as making people responsible for their own spiritual growth. We provide the environment for them to grow. We offer tools to help them grow. And we hope to motivate and inspire them to grow. But the task of the pastor is not to spoon-feed the faithful the secret truths of the faith.

But beyond that, what I really want you to know is this: There are no secret truths! There is no spiritual giant out there who has this figured out, while the rest of us are bumbling in the dark. It is just not that complicated. Jesus summarized spirituality with two commands: Love God and love your neighbor. John Wesley and the early Methodists summarized it in three "general rules": Avoid doing the things you know are wrong. Do good to everyone that you can, as often as you can. And pursue those practices that encourage you in the faith and draw you near to God—practices like prayer, reading the Bible, attending worship, fast-

What I really want you to know is this: There are no secret truths! There is no spiritual giant out there who has this figured out, while the rest of us are bumbling in the dark. It is just not that complicated.

ing, and meeting with other Christians to help one another grow.

Whole books have been written on the spiritual life. I'm not trying to minimize their value. What I am trying to say is that, on the one hand, there are no deep secrets or silver bullets that you'll read in a book or find at someone else's church. There is this journey of daily seeking to love God, of loving your neighbor, and doing those things that help you grow to be like Christ. And you will have moments where you are doing really well. And times where you feel the peace and joy and hope. But there will also be moments where you struggle, and times where God seems like nothing more than a myth.

One of my favorite books on the spiritual life is Mike Yaconelli's *Messy Spirituality*. Listen to how he describes his own spiritual life,

> My life is a mess. After forty-five years of trying to follow Jesus, I keep losing him in the crowded busyness of my life. . . . For as long as I can remember, I have wanted to be a godly person. Yet when I look at the yesterdays of my life, what I see, mostly, is a broken, irregular path littered with mistakes and failure . . . I want desperately to know God better. I want to be consistent, but right now the only consistency in my life is my inconsistency . . . I want to have more victories than defeats, yet here I am, almost sixty, and I fail on a regular basis.[2]

That's honest, and that is how the spiritual life works. We take two steps forward, and sometimes *three* back. We have a yearning for more, which keeps us seeking more, and that is a good thing. I think the Holy Spirit actually places that desire for more within us. But that has to be balanced with a knowledge that the spiritual life, as long as we are on this earth, will be a journey in which we'll have moments and glimpses of this wonderful, amazing reality, but these will eventually fade, and then we'll struggle, we'll falter, and we'll sometimes feel afraid.

And somehow, that's OK. We keep waking up each day, seeking to follow, committing our lives to God, praying a little, reading a little, worshiping a little, serving others, showing compassion, opening our lives to the Spirit's work. And we keep yearning to grow.

Part of what I love about the Bible is that it allows us to see that even the heroes of the faith struggled. Abraham gave away Sarah twice, pretending she was his sister, just to save his own skin. Moses killed a man, whined a lot, and didn't always follow God's commands carefully. David gives me the greatest hope for my spiritual life. If a man can commit adultery, and commit murder, and still be a "friend of God," I feel encouraged that there's hope for me! Then there's Peter, who denied Jesus, and Thomas who struggled with doubt, and James and John who were still debating about which of them Jesus liked more, while Jesus prepared to be crucified. There's Paul, whose confession in Romans 7 about his own spiritual struggles describes in such powerful detail my own spiritual life so many times. And there are so many more. They all struggled. And yet they are the heroes of our faith.

Among my favorite descriptions of the spiritual life is the poem written from a Nazi concentration camp by pastor and theologian Dietrich Bonhoeffer. What I love is his sheer honesty. This man risked everything to pursue the kingdom of God and to try to put an end to Hitler's murderous reign. He would be put to

> Part of what I love about the Bible is that it allows us to see that even the heroes of the faith struggled.

death days before the Allies liberated his camp. But even this man, whose faith and witness continue to speak sixty years after his death, felt the tension, glimpsing at times what the spiritual life could be, and often feeling a failure in pursuing it. The poem is called "Who Am I?" In it, Bonhoeffer describes the contrast between how others saw him in the concentration camp—as one who was calm and cheerful and friendly and confident—and the man he felt he was on the inside, "trembling with anger at despotisms and petty humiliation . . . weary and empty at praying, at thinking, at making, faint and ready to say farewell to it all." He wonders if he is a hypocrite to others and a weakling to himself. But he ends this powerful poem with these words of affirmation, "Who am I? They mock me, these lonely questions of mine. Whoever I am, Thou knowest, O God, I am thine."[3]

There are no secrets. There's struggle, and yearning, and doing the things we know we should do. And in the end, there is trust. *Whoever I am, Thou knowest, O God, I am thine.*

Notes

1. *Messy Spirituality* (Grand Rapids, Mich.: Zondervan, 2002), 11.
2. Ibid., page 10.
3. Now published as *Who Am I* (Minneapolis: Augsburg, 2005). I first read the poem in the introduction to earlier editions of *The Cost of Discipleship*.

Part III
Politics and Ethics in the Center

Our political leadership has been at its best when those leaders have dared to enter into the world of gray. . . . It requires far less courage to live in the black and white than it does to live in the gray. The world of gray requires that we show up and be present. It does not afford us the luxury of putting life on automatic pilot.

—Byron Williams[1]

Seventeen
Situation Ethics and WWJD

"I give you a new commandment, that you love one another.
Just as I have loved you, you also should love one another. By this
everyone will know that you are my disciples, if you have love for
one another."
—John 13:34-35

In 1966, Joseph Fletcher, an Episcopal priest at the time, and professor of Christian ethics at Cambridge, wrote his landmark book *Situation Ethics: The New Morality*. Fletcher was not necessarily creating a new ethic, but rather was giving voice to what had been an ethical approach or form of ethical reasoning that had been practiced by human beings throughout history.

He attempted to find a middle way between legalism (a rules-based ethical system with absolute rules always to be followed) and antinomianism or libertinism (which said that there were no moral absolutes, meaning that each individual was to follow his or her own conscience and that what really mattered were outcomes). Fletcher recognized that simply following absolute rules did not take into account the complexity and variety of situations in which moral decisions must be made and that, at times, the absolutes themselves could become the source of evil. At the same time he recognized the need for some kind of absolute that might guide Christians toward the right answer in all circumstances.

Fletcher proposed that Jesus' second great commandment, the commandment to love one's

Fletcher suggested that, in every situation, one question could lead us to the right path: What is the loving thing to do?

147

neighbor, was the one moral absolute upon which all ethical decisions could be based. He suggested that, in every situation, one question could lead us to the right path: What is the loving thing to do? Jesus indicated that love was the essence of all the Law and the Prophets. Twice Paul notes that this commandment is the summary of all the others. James called this the "royal law" (James 2:8). In 1 Corinthians 13:13 Paul notes that of the fundamental principles of faith, hope, and love, "the greatest of these is love." First John 4:7-8 tells us that God *is* love. These all point to love as the guiding principle of Christian ethics.

My aim in this chapter is neither to give a comprehensive summary of Fletcher's views, nor to defend or critique them as an adequate basis for Christian ethics. I don't believe situation ethics as articulated by Fletcher offers a completely satisfactory approach to making moral decisions, and that elements of Fletcher's thought are open to considerable criticism. Among the places where situation ethics breaks down is its requirement that each individual be capable of discerning what the loving thing to do is—and this is difficult for us, in part because we are broken; our sin nature tends to lead us to justify evil as good and loving. But I think Fletcher's work invites us to think about rules and moral absolutes in ways that might be helpful as we are seeking to find a middle ground between conservativism and liberalism.

It also seems to me that some kind of situation ethics is clearly evidenced in the Bible itself. Allow me to illustrate: Imagine four different men, each of whom used a gun to kill another man. In each case we have a killer, a weapon, and a dead victim. Yet imagine with me that one is a police officer firing in self-defense. The second is a soldier on the front lines of a just war. The third is a complete accident—the man holding the weapon picked up the gun and it accidentally discharged and the bullet ricocheted off the sidewalk, striking and killing another man. And finally, the last of these men carefully planned the murder of one of his enemies. Have all four done the same thing, even though they each used a gun and each killed another? In fact, not only in the Old Testament, but in contemporary law as well, one of these men may be a hero, another will not spend a day in jail for he fired in self-defense. Another will be found guilty of the lesser crime of involuntary manslaughter. And another will be found guilty of murder. What is the difference between murder, manslaughter, war, and self-defense? The difference is motive, intent, and the particular situation. The Old Testament, as well as our own justice system, recognizes a difference among each of these.

Let's begin with a simple question: How do you decide what is right and wrong? Not long ago everywhere you turned someone would be wearing a bracelet with these four letters, WWJD, standing for What Would Jesus Do? Those who wore these bracelets presumably used this question in much the same way that Fletcher encouraged us to ask, What is the loving thing to do? It became a guiding principle for daily life. Its simplicity and the mental imagery of thinking about Jesus walking in our shoes, and imagining what he would do, was very helpful for many people. This was, itself, a kind of situation ethics. The guiding principle was Jesus. The wearer would ask, In this particular situation, what would Jesus do?

How do you decide what is right and wrong?

The challenge is knowing for certain what Jesus would do. Is it up to each individual believer to imagine what Jesus would do based upon his or her preconceived ideas of Jesus, or is there more we can look at to guide us to the answer to this question? A second question we might ask is: Just because Jesus would do something, or refrain from doing something, should we expect that he would require that we do the same?[2]

Just because Jesus would do something, or refrain from doing something, should we expect that he would require that we do the same?

Nevertheless, even though this form of situation ethics breaks down, it still is a helpful device for thinking about how Jesus' followers should live. In the same way, Fletcher's question, "What is the loving thing to do in this situation?" can give us moral and ethical guidance in daily living, despite the fact that it breaks down as the only guide for how we live.

Fortunately, we are not left on our own to determine what Jesus would do, or what act might fulfill his law of love. We have numerous resources to help us live lives that would please God. The first of these is Scripture. The Bible records the sayings of Jesus, and his deeds.[3] The New Testament contains the reflections of the early Christians on what it meant to follow Jesus and how we might love our neighbor as we love ourselves. In addition to the Scriptures, we have the tradition of the Christian church through the centuries: the reflections and ethical reasoning of people of faith for two thousand years. Ethical ideas like just war theory come from the church's reflection of the Scriptures and attempts to relate its principles to specific situations.

God has also given us the church community—our friends in small groups and Sunday school, our pastors, and teachers— to help us discern what Jesus would do or how we are to live the law of love in specific situations. At times when I have been uncertain about the right course of action to take, I was grateful for my friends in Christ who God used to help me think about which action to take. The wisdom they provided as together we prayed about thorny issues, or confusing and multifaceted problems, allowed me to make better decisions than I ever would have made on my own. John Wesley spoke of this as Christian conferencing.

Methodists speak of the Wesleyan Quadrilateral[4] that guides our theological and ethical reflections: Scripture, tradition, experience, and reason. Scripture is primary; tradition secondary; experience is specifically the Holy Spirit's direct witness to our hearts; and reason, which Methodist theologians placed last as subject to the others, is still a critical gift God gave us so that we might be able to discern what is right.

For all its weaknesses, the power of the situation ethics approach (WWJD or What is the loving thing to do?) is that it recognizes that each individual situation varies from another and that the challenge in applying absolute laws is that there are situations to which the absolute laws simply cannot apply. This approach seems to me more in keeping with the promise of God in Jeremiah 31:33 to write his law on our hearts. It seems more consistent with the words of Paul we studied in the last chapter from Galatians, calling us to live by the Spirit.

In the end I believe Fletcher missed the mark in emphasizing only the second of the two great commandments. Together the two great commandments are meant to guide our lives. They are the moral absolutes that guide our response in every situation. We are to ask first, What course of action could I take that would express my love for God? And second, What is the most loving thing to do toward my neighbor? There are moral situations where my actions will not in any way hurt a neighbor, but this is not the only criterion that guides our lives. For what may not hurt my neighbor may in fact bring offense or grief to God.

There are a host of things I seek to avoid in life not because participating in them would harm anyone else, but because I don't believe they would honor and please God. There are courses of action I take in my life with an eye toward honoring God and expressing my love and devotion to him, though they have no direct bearing, good or bad, on another human being.

Every morning as I begin my day I slip to my knees next to my bed and pray. After opening words of praise, an act of confession, words of thanksgiving for the blessings in my life, and petitions for my family and others, I say this: "Lord, help me to honor you today. In every meeting, in every chance encounter, in every decision, and in every word, help me to express my love for you, and

151

your love for others." Some variation of that prayer is meant to guide us as we aim to live our lives each day.

It is in holding together the two great commandments, and seeking in every situation to pursue them, that we find a powerful guiding force for our lives. In every situation we ask, What course of action will best express my love for God and neighbor? And we are not left to our own devices in trying to answer these questions. God has given us the resources of our intellect for moral reasoning, our experience of the Holy Spirit's witness in our lives, the blessing of Christian community—both our friends today and the tradition of the church through the generations—and the gift of Holy Scripture.

> In every situation we ask, What course of action will best express my love for God and neighbor?

What situation ethics and the popular contemporary version of it—WWJD—offer is an invitation to find that place between a morality simply based upon rules (legalism) and a morality without rules, based simply on the desire of the individual (libertinism). It reminds us that, in every situation, we are called to seek to do God's will by fulfilling the law of love.

Notes

1. Byron Williams, "Black and White Thinking Doesn't Work in a Gray World," *The Huffington Post*, October 2, 2006.
2. For instance, Jesus stood in the temple courts and denounced the religious leaders for their hypocrisy, yet he told the people to obey the Pharisees, only being careful to not do as they did. Jesus didn't marry. He would not have bought a home, a car, or a television set. Does this preclude us from doing so?
3. The words and the deeds of Jesus must go hand in hand. What he does helps us interpret what he says. For instance, Jesus tells us in the Sermon on the Mount that divorce, except for infidelity, is sin. But in John 4 we read the story of Jesus' encounter with a woman who had been divorced five times. The teaching and the encounter must be taken together as the church formulates its response to divorced persons.
4. Anglican tradition speaks of a three-legged stool of Scripture, tradition, and reason—to which Wesley and his followers added the dimension of the experience of the Holy Spirit.

Eighteen
Abortion: Finding Common Ground

*Americans cannot be easily characterized as conservative or
liberal on today's most pressing social questions. . . . Along with
favoring no clear ideological approach to most social issues, the
public expresses a desire for a middle ground on the most divisive
social concern of the day: abortion.*
—*Summary of a 2006 Pew Forum on Religion and Public
Life Survey of 2003 Americans*

No other controversial issue is as emotionally charged or has
the capacity to generate such deep-seated feelings of anger
and indignation as abortion. The poles in this case are clear. They
may go by different names, but we most often hear the designations pro-life and pro-choice. Those most passionate about the
issue on either side seem to see little or no room for compromise.

When it comes to the debate about abortion I am reminded of
Newton's Third Law of Motion: "For every action there is an equal
and opposite reaction." You've seen this law illustrated, no doubt,
with the use of a toy called the Newton's cradle—five silver balls
suspended by wires or string between a frame. When one ball is
pulled back and released, it strikes the remaining four balls, sending the last of them flying back to a distance roughly equivalent to
the distance from which the first ball was dropped. This action-
reaction of the Newton's cradle is the picture I have of the pro-life
and pro-choice movements in America.[1] For thirty years each side
has sought to gain the upper hand, and each law that is passed,
each proposition that is put forth, seems to generate an equal and
opposite law or proposition on the part of the opposing force. In
the process there is a lot of "heat" but very little "light" produced
in the debate.

My aim in this chapter is not to recount the arguments in the debate. I have laid out the moral arguments on both sides of this issue and my own moral reasoning on it in my book *Confronting the Controversies*.[2] My hope is to offer a constructive approach for moving forward.

My assumption is that we will never come to a place in America where we have agreement on this issue. According to the most recent polling, slightly more than half of Americans surveyed believed that abortion should always or usually be legal.[3] This meant that slightly fewer than half felt abortion should be illegal in most cases. A strong majority of respondents opposed late-term abortions. When questioned as to whether abortion should be legal in the case of rape, incest, or when the life of the mother is at risk, a majority of those who are pro-life believed abortion should be legal. Yet 13 percent of those surveyed believed abortion should be illegal, even when it would be necessary to save the life of a woman.[4] In 2006 the Pew Research Center conducted a poll asking, "When it comes to abortion policy do you believe, (a) We need to find a middle ground, or (b) There is no room for compromise on this issue." Fifty-five percent of Americans responded that there is a need to find a middle ground, with only 29 percent believing there was no room for compromise.[5] My aim in this chapter is to suggest some ways in which a middle ground might be found.

> My assumption is that we will never come to a place in America where we have agreement on [the issue of abortion]. My aim, however, is to suggest some ways in which a middle ground might be found.

I'd like to begin by considering the poles in this debate over abortion.

PRO-CHOICE   PRO-LIFE

X   X

The most extreme positions can be summarized as follows. On the pro-choice side, the fetus is not seen as a human being until it has been delivered and it is no longer dependent upon the life of the mother for support. Only then does it gain rights. Up to the point of delivery the mother should have a legal right to abort the fetus. This position would be held by a very small percentage of those who support abortion rights.

The most extreme pro-life position would hold that from the moment of conception the conceptus is a human being who possesses a soul, *and* that the fertilized egg (and, as it develops, the fetus) cannot be willfully destroyed or aborted, not even to save the life of the mother. As noted above, 13 percent of respondents indicated that abortion should not be allowed under any circumstances, even in the case of an effort to save a woman's life. A very small number of the most ardent pro-life advocates have even supported the use of violence to stop doctors from performing abortions.[6]

These views represent the poles in the debate over abortion. But the vast majority of those who are pro-life or pro-choice do not identify with the extremes.

Of those who identify themselves as pro-choice, the majority oppose late-term abortions. Of those who are pro-life, the majority would allow for a legal abortion in the event of rape, incest, or to protect the health of the mother.[7] Further, in speaking with women and men who identify themselves as pro-choice, it is not uncommon to hear them state that "I would not personally have an abortion, but I believe that there are situations in which a woman should have the legal ability to have an abortion." Many of these persons would agree with pro-choice advocate William Saletan's January 22, 2006, Op-Ed piece in *The New York Times* in which he wrote: "Abortion is bad, and the ideal number of abortions is zero." He noted that "abortion . . . generates moral friction. Most people will tolerate it as a lesser evil or a temporary measure, but they'll never fully accept it. They want a world in which it's less necessary."[8] If this is, in fact, where a majority of pro-choice advocates find themselves, this would indicate that many are already much closer to the center than the polls often indicate. The continuum pointing out where a majority of pro-life and pro-choice advocates are likely looks more like this:

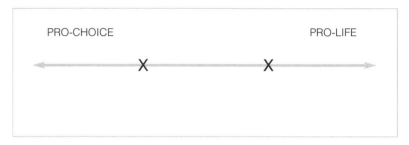

I believe the majority of people in America would find their position represented near these two Xs. When seen this way it begins to seem at least possible that the two sides in this debate might be able to find common ground and work together to achieve common goals as Saletan suggested in his Op-Ed piece.

According to the Guttmacher Institute, 46 percent of women who have abortions in the United States each year were not using birth control when they became pregnant. Understanding and addressing the reasons for the failure to use birth control could reduce the number of abortions by more than 500,000 each year. [9] If both pro-choice and pro-life advocates could agree that birth control is preferable to abortion, and work together on this approach, the goals of both would be partially achieved.

Many pro-life advocates prefer encouraging abstinence for unmarried persons to birth control. Some pro-choice advocates also recognize the value of abstinence. What if, as a nation, we sought to reclaim the sense of the sacredness of sex among young people? What if both liberals and conservatives came together to try to influence society's view of sex with serious advertising campaigns while seeking to enlist Hollywood in an effort to reshape an entire generation regarding the meaning and sanctity of sexual intercourse—to see it is as something beautiful, holy, and which is meant to bind two people together in the most profound of ways? What if we moved away from portraying sex as something everyone does after only a couple of dates and sought to shift away from the glorifying of casual or recreational sex? Is it possible this, too,

> One does not need to be conservative to believe that sexual intimacy is something profound, that the sharing of one's body with another human being is supposed to be meaningful. This might be a place for the right and the left to seek agreement.

would reduce the number of abortions? One does not need to be conservative to believe that sexual intimacy is something profound, that the sharing of one's body with another human being is supposed to be meaningful. This might be a place for the right and the left to seek agreement.

Seventy percent of all women having abortions in the United States identify themselves as Christians: 43 percent are Protestant and 27 percent are Roman Catholic.[10] Given the fact that there will be debate in society at large regarding the time when the claims of the fetus to be born are greater than the claim of the mother to exercise complete control over her own body, I think it is unlikely that *Roe v. Wade* will be overturned. But if 70 percent of those having abortions claim to be Christian, the church must, with compassion and love, articulate to its members the reasons they should choose to carry a child to term when the pregnancy is unplanned—and then the church must plan to support such women. This is a catch-22 for some churches, particularly when the woman is unmarried. Would supporting the woman mean dismissing the fact that she conceived outside of marriage? If the church is serious about reducing abortions, it must (and I think most do) find ways to remove the stigma surrounding a woman conceiving out of wedlock.

> The church must, with compassion and love, articulate to its members the reasons they should choose to carry a child to term when the pregnancy is unplanned—and then the church must plan to support such women.

I believe there is room, between the poles,

for most pro-life and pro-choice advocates to find at least some middle ground where they might work together to accomplish common goals of reducing the number of abortions. I would like to suggest seven points upon which I believe moderate pro-life and moderate pro-choice advocates could agree:

1. Pro-choice advocates and pro-life advocates each have legitimate concerns.
2. Abortion is both "not ideal" and yet, occasionally, "necessary" (at the very least, most pro-life advocates would allow abortion to save the life of the mother).
3. Decreasing the number of abortions in America would be desirable.
4. Adequate information about and access to birth control can reduce abortions.
5. The longer a pregnancy progresses the more morally problematic an abortion becomes.
6. No one should be pressured into having an abortion.
7. If an abortion occurs it should be safe.

There is a place for pro-choice and pro-life advocates to sit down with one another, in a spirit of humility, and with a willingness to listen in order to understand the other's concerns. If they do this, there is an opportunity to see if they can find shared strategies for reducing the number of unwanted pregnancies and abortions each year.

Our society has made abortions legal under far wider circumstances than many Christians find morally justifiable. Given that abortions will occur for reasons some will find morally objectionable, and that it seems unlikely that *Roe v. Wade* will be entirely overturned, it behooves those who are pro-life to seek ways to foster efforts by both sides in this debate to reduce the situations in which abortions are sought.

If a pregnancy is to be terminated, I favor the use of what is commonly called "the morning-after pill" or "emergency contraception" rather than allowing the embryo to develop and be aborted later. These pills prohibit the fertilized egg from implanting in the uterus and they are effective up to three days after unprotected sex. I support this as an alternative to surgical abortions, recognizing that surgical abortions might not take place until weeks five to twelve of the pregnancy, by which time the heart begins to beat and development progresses rapidly. If an abortion is going to occur, it seems to me morally preferable to end a pregnancy at the stage when many pregnancies are, in nature, terminated (some estimate that as much as 40 percent of the time when women conceive, the fertilized egg does not implant in the uterus, it is sloughed off, and the woman never knows she had conceived[11]) and when there is only a collection of undifferentiated cells.

I believe conception is a miraculous event in which we have become cocreators with God, and is to be violated only under the most extreme of situations. While for many women who seek abortion, this decision is traumatic and not taken lightly, the number of repeat abortions would indicate that for many, abortion has become a form of birth control and the act of ending the life of a developing human being is not taken seriously enough. I believe this diminishes the humanity of the individuals seeking abortions, and the rest of society as well.

A letter I received from one of my parishioners seven years ago has fundamentally shaped how I view abortion. The woman wrote and told me that she was seventeen and her boyfriend was sixteen when they had sex for the first time. It only took one time for her to conceive.

She told me how, when her father found out about the pregnancy, he was furious. These were the days before *Roe v. Wade* and legal elective abortions were not available. So he set up an appointment with a doctor in Switzerland. He would fly her there for the procedure. But she refused to go. She and the boy were going to marry and have the baby. She writes, "My father told me I would never be welcome in his home again if I went through with the marriage and delivery of the baby."

She moved in with the boy's family and the couple quickly married. They dropped out of high school in order to care for this child. The couple struggled over the next few years, barely making ends meet. After twelve years their marriage ended in divorce. This couple's future was radically changed by their decision to have the baby. For both the woman, who gave birth, and her young husband, their childhood was cut short; they did not go to college, and ultimately they divorced. I wondered if this woman regretted her decision. But her letter concluded in this way:

> Yes, my life changed dramatically due to the pregnancy prior to marriage but, to this day, that child has been the greatest blessing to me and thousands of others. God prompts him to call his Mom when she needs to talk but doesn't want to bother him. God has blessed me more with this son than I can ever imagine being blessed. I am so proud of the Husband and Father that he has become. So many times when I look at him I think that this . . . person could have ended up aborted, but instead, due to the classes in Sunday School week after week that had been taught to me as a child, I knew that even from the very moment that he was conceived, he was a gift from God. I look back sometimes at the college that I missed, the experiences that "could have been" . . . my life is different than it could have been but I wouldn't change it for anything.
>
> Thank you, Adam, for being my "gift from God"—there can be no greater gift than that of a child that God wants to be born. I never dreamed 36 years ago while I was carrying you that you would have the impact on God's people, and me, that you do. You are my Pastor, my confidant and my best friend.
>
> I love you, Mom

This is *my mother's* story, and *I* am that child. And what it reminds me of is a powerful gospel truth: God takes what we think of as "mistakes" and "accidents" and redeems them. This is what he specializes in. He knits us together in our mothers' wombs—he has plans for each child. These "accidents" and "unwanted babies" have potential. They grow up. I am one of those children. And had abortion been as readily available and accepted in 1964 as it is today, my mother may have aborted me.

There are complex moral situations in which there are "tragic conflicts of life with life." In those situations there needs to be a legal and safe option for abortion. Yet our society has embraced a very broad understanding of when abortion is appropriate. Christians, both liberal and conservative, should be asking critical questions about when the removal and destruction of a forming human being from the

> Both those who are pro-choice and those who are pro-life can and should agree that the number of abortions is too high, and that it should be reduced.

womb is morally acceptable. Over one million abortions occur in the United States each year. At least 75 percent of these are unrelated to the health of the mother, the health of the fetus, rape, or incest. [12] Both those who are pro-choice and those who are pro-life can and should agree that this number is too high, and that it should be reduced. And it is important to note that thirty-five years of heated rhetoric and court battles have not led to a significant reduction in the number of abortions. Both sides must move beyond the current impasse. Only as pro-life and pro-choice advocates work together, understanding the concerns of the other, and looking for solutions to address one another's concerns, will abortion become increasingly rare in our society, and that seems a goal that both sides could agree upon.

Notes

1. The Newton's cradle is an interesting metaphor I've used to describe what happens in politics in America, and in the broader culture wars as a whole, where so much of what we see happening is reactionary, and those in the center tend to get "hit" by those on both sides.
2. *Confronting the Controversies* (Nashville: Abingdon, 2005). This book is also available as a small-group study with a fifteen-minute video in which I summarize the various issues covered by each chapter. A leader's guide is also available. The chapters cover topics such as the separation of church and

state, prayer in public schools, euthanasia, the death penalty, abortion, and homosexuality, among others.

3. I reviewed the data from six different nationwide polls concerning abortion that were conducted in the spring and summer of 2007. The data can be found at www.pollingreport.com/abortion.htm.

4. This information is from the NBC News/*Wall Street Journal* Poll conducted April 20–23, 2007, in which 1,004 adults responded. I believe the question was not carefully worded—it would have been more helpful to discover how many would support abortion in the case of rape, then how many would support legal abortion in the case of incest, and finally, how many would support legal abortion in the case of the life of the woman being at risk. The results in the poll showed that 55 percent of those surveyed believed that the decision for abortion should be made between a woman and her doctor. This was understood to be support for legalized abortion. An additional 30 percent of respondents supported the legal option of abortion in the case of rape or incest or when the life of the woman was at risk. Thirteen percent responded that abortion should always be illegal. Since approximately 45 percent of the population surveyed in other polls taken in the spring identified themselves as pro-life it would appear that the majority of those considering themselves pro-life support a legal option for abortion in these circumstances.

5. The survey interviewed 2,003 adults between July 6–19, 2006. See http://pew forum.org/publications/surveys/social-issues-06.pdf.

6. For an example of the moral reasoning of those who advocate killing abortion doctors, see the "Eulogy for Paul Hill" by Rev. Bruce Evan Murch found at www.covenantnews.com/murch030905.htm. For links to numerous websites of more radical pro-life groups and proponents see www.my.execpc.com/~awal lace/index.htm.

7. The data for the percentage of abortions that occur for these three reasons, plus fetal deformity, vary significantly by survey, but appear to be between 2 and 10 percent of all abortions performed.

8. William Saletan, "Three Decades After Roe, a War We Can All Support," *The New York Times*, January 22, 2006. The piece can be read online at www.nytimes.com/2006/01/22/opinion/22saletan.html?ex=1187236800&en= 29ef0966e859ed15&ei=5070.

9. See www.guttmacher.org/pubs/fb_induced_abortion.html. The figure of 500,000 plus abortions that would be avoided is derived from multiplying the 46% of abortions that occur among women not using contraceptives times the total number of induced abortions of 1.29 million that occurred in 2002 as cited by Guttmacher, which gives a total of 593,000 abortions that could be averted if all contraceptives were used by these women. Given the unlikelihood of all of these women using birth control, and the small but known failure rate of birth control, increased use of contraceptives could

nevertheless still result in a reduction in abortions in the hundreds of thousands each year.

10. Ibid.

11. The 40 percent figure for zygotes which do not implant in naturally occurring fertilizations is widely reported. See Gregory Pence, *Re Creating Medicine: Ethical Issues at the Frontiers of Medicine* (Rowman & Littlefield, 2007), 124, among many others. The range of numbers given for this is typically between 30 and 50 percent.

12. A 2005 Guttmacher Institute study entitled, "Reasons U.S. Women Have Abortions: Quantitative and Qualitative Perspectives" by Finer, et. al. can be read online at www.guttmacher.org/pubs/psrh/full/3711005.pdf. It offers the results of a 2004 survey that indicated that 13 percent of surveyed women who had abortions did so, in part, for concern for the fetus' health, and 12 percent in part out of concern for the woman's own health. National Right to Life suggests that the number is actually 8 percent and that the Guttmacher study revealed that 92 percent of women had abortions for reasons other than protecting the woman's health or the fetus's health. See "New Study Examines Reasons Women Have Abortions" by Randall O'Bannon and found at www.nrlc.org/news/2005/NRL10/NewStudy.html.

Nineteen
Homosexuality at the Center

*My church's exclusion of homosexuals who confess Christ and
live together in committed love makes me very sad. . . . Is there really a wideness in God's mercy like the wideness of the sea? Is his
mercy wide enough for people who, through no choice of their own,
have no other way to fulfill one of the deepest of all human needs
but the way that my wife and I have fulfilled them for fifty years—
in an abiding partnership of lasting love? I think I know my own
heart well enough to believe that if his mercy is wide enough for me,
it must be wide enough for them.*
—Lewis Smedes[1]

In the spring of 2000 I was a reserve delegate to The United
Methodist Church's General Conference, held once every four
years. I was sitting in the balcony when the issue of homosexuality was being debated by the church. Outside the Cleveland Convention Center, Fred Phelps and his followers had protested
earlier, holding their signs as we filed past: "God Hates Fags!" "Fag
Church UMC," and others. At this particular session demonstra-
tors who sought to end The United Methodist Church's ban on ordination for self-avowed, practicing homosexuals, and who hoped
the church would remove language critical of homosexual practice from its *Discipline*, entered the convention center, surrounding the delegates by standing on the perimeter of the room, both
on the main floor and the balcony to silently watch as The United
Methodist Church voted on the issue of our official position on
homosexuality. Following the church's vote to maintain our current prohibitions against homosexual marriage and the ordination
of homosexuals, and retaining the language that stated that the

165

practice of homosexuality was "incompatible with Christian teaching" these persons began to file onto the floor where the delegates sat. Others came to the balcony and stood in a ring around the balcony. A woman came and stood at the end of the aisle in my section, directly in front of me, looking down upon the delegates twenty-five feet below. She was shaking and visibly distraught. Soon she climbed up onto the edge of the balcony, and she stood there, looking over the floor of the conference, looking at the people who had just voted once again to exclude her from full participation in the church, and she began to shout at them. I could not understand what she was saying, but I sensed that she might be planning to jump. I stepped out of my seat, along with another, and quickly reached for the woman just as she began to leap. We pulled her back down into our laps, and held her as she lay shaking. We held her in our arms until a few moments later, when a friend arrived to care for her and walk her out. The entire incident took place in a matter of seconds, but the impact upon me, and others at the conference, still lingers.

In the spring of 2004, on the weekend before The United Methodist Church was preparing to meet once again for its General Conference, I decided I needed to preach on the issue of homosexuality. Our people would be hearing about the church's deliberations in the press. I wanted them to understand the debate from me, their pastor. I also wanted to spend time wrestling with this issue once again myself. I began preparing for this sermon assuming it would be basically the same message that appears in the 2001 edition of my book *Confronting the Controversies*. One thing I had invited people to do in preparation for this new sermon was to send me

> Reading these stories [related to homosexuality] of real people in our congregation, and trying to discern what Jesus would say and do if he were preaching this sermon, led me to a place of tremendous inner turmoil.

their own stories related to homosexuality—whether they were homosexual, had once considered themselves homosexual but no longer did so, or had family members who were homosexuals. I received more than one hundred responses from people in our congregation. Reading these stories of real people in our congregation, and trying to discern what Jesus would say and do if he were preaching this sermon, led me to a place of tremendous inner turmoil. Had I not announced the previous week that I would be preaching on this subject, I would likely have changed topics. What you are about to read is the text of that sermon from 2004.

In the twelve months following the preaching of this sermon, hundreds of people left our church. Many were people I had baptized, cared for, and loved. They felt I had not "held the line" on homosexuality. A handful left because they felt I had not been open enough to gays and lesbians, but most left because they felt I had "drifted" to the left on this issue. It was painful for them, for our church, and for me. I had doubts about my ministry and whether somehow I had let God down. In the years since I have spent hundreds of hours reading, writing, and praying about this issue, continuing to wrestle with the biblical ideal that God created us male and female, and the reality of the world in which we live, where five percent of the population seems to be wired differently from heterosexuals and where this population has often been wounded by the church.[2]

I am convinced that the Christian church—not just the mainline, but also the conservative and evangelical

> I am convinced that the Christian church—not just the mainline, but also the conservative and evangelical churches—will struggle with this issue, and that in the coming decades all but the most conservative of churches will have come to grips with this topic in some way that looks more gray than black and white.

churches—will struggle with this issue, and that in the coming decades all but the most conservative of churches will have come to grips with this topic in some way that looks more gray than black and white. I am not yet sure what that looks like. One final aside: While we lost hundreds of members in the year following my preaching the sermon that follows, we had more than 1,000 people who joined the church during that same period of time.

A Sermon on Homosexuality

Introduction:
Scripture and Tradition on Homosexuality

Homosexuality is an important issue to reflect upon. And it is not going away. I believe in the decades ahead society will look at homosexuality in a way not dissimilar to how we look at divorce today. Homosexual unions of one kind or another will be widely available, and you will be working with people who are in these relationships. Some will be your children or grandchildren, nieces or nephews, or the children of your closest friends.

My aim today is not to persuade you which side to take on this issue. Many of you already know what you believe and nothing I could say would change your minds. What I hope to do is help you better understand both your own position and the position of those with whom you disagree.

I am going to begin by sharing with you the scriptures usually quoted as having some relevance for the question of homosexuality. Then I am going to summarize what our tradition—The United Methodist Church—says about homosexuality in our *Book of Discipline*. This week, our denomination's leaders will gather for General Conference where they will be debating changes to our current position. In today's message I will summarize the arguments of the progressives, who want to remove language branding homosexual practice a sin. I will then summarize the arguments of those who are traditionalists, who wish to retain this language. After summarizing these two positions, I will share with you some of the things you, our members, said to me in the last week or two as you sent me over one hundred e-mails and letters telling me your stories. Finally I will share with you where I stand.

A. *The Biblical Passages Specifically Mentioning Some Form of Same-Sex Practice*

Let's begin by examining the scriptures most often quoted as forbidding homosexuality.

The first is found in Genesis 19:1-29, where we find a story of two messengers from God who came as strangers to the town of Sodom where Lot lived. The men from that town demanded that Lot surrender these messengers to them, and they intended to sexually assault them. Here, and in a similar story in Judges 19, some would say the issue is not primarily about homosexuality—it is about evil and power and rape. In ancient times, as in some places today, a man would sexually victimize another man as a way of demonstrating superiority and dominion over him, and by extension, over his people. Those who did this did not generally consider themselves

In ancient times, as in some places today, a man would sexually victimize another man as a way of demonstrating superiority and dominion over him, and by extension, over his people. Those who did this did not generally consider themselves homosexuals, but men who were asserting their superiority over other men by using and abusing them.

homosexuals, but men who were asserting their superiority over other men by using and abusing them.

The next two passages are directly about homosexual intimacy. Leviticus 18:22 and 20:13 come from that section of the Law of Moses known as the Purity or Holiness Code. Leviticus 18:22 reads "You shall not lie with a male as with a woman; it is an abomination." And Leviticus 20:13 reads "If a man lies with a male as with a woman, both of them have committed an abomination; they shall be put to death; their blood is upon them." We'll discuss these further in a moment.

In the New Testament there are three passages usually quoted regarding homosexual practices. First Corinthians 6:9-10 mentions "male prostitutes" and "sodomites" (the NIV calls them "homosexual offenders"), alongside the drunkards and the greedy and says of them that they will not inherit the kingdom of God. First Timothy 1:10 mentions "sodomites" alongside liars and those engaged in sex outside of marriage as lawless and disobedient. Again, we'll consider how these are read by the progressives and traditionalists in a moment.[3]

Finally, and considered the most pertinent scriptures regarding homosexual practice, are Romans 1:23-27, which are a part of a larger passage. We read:

> They . . . exchanged the glory of the immortal God for images resembling a mortal human being or birds or four-footed animals or reptiles.
>
> Therefore God gave them up in the lusts of their hearts to impurity, to the degrading of their bodies among themselves, because they exchanged the truth about God for a lie and worshiped and served the creature rather than the Creator, who is blessed for ever! Amen.
>
> For this reason God gave them up to degrading passions. Their women exchanged natural intercourse for unnatural, and in the same way also the men, giving up natural intercourse with women, were consumed with passion for one another. Men committed shameless acts with men and received in their own persons the due penalty for their error.

B. *The Current United Methodist Position:*
Book of Discipline (2000)

Now that you are familiar with *every* passage in the Bible that directly mentions anything approximating homosexual acts, let's turn to the tradition of our denomination. What does The United Methodist Church officially teach regarding homosexuality? Well, it's a bit of a mixed bag. Our *Book of Discipline* states in its Social Principles, paragraph 162H:

> We are committed to supporting [civil rights] for homosexual persons. We see a clear issue of simple justice in protecting their rightful claims where they have shared material resources, pensions, guardian relationships, mutual powers of attorney, and other such lawful claims . . . moreover, we support efforts to stop violence and other forms of coercion against gays and lesbians.

In paragraph 161G we read:

> Homosexual persons no less than heterosexual persons are individuals of sacred worth. All persons need the ministry and guidance of the church in their struggle for human fulfillment, as well as the spiritual and emotional care of a fellowship. Although we do not condone the practice of homosexuality and consider this practice incompatible with Christian teaching, we affirm that God's grace is available to all.

In paragraph 304.3 we read:

> Since the practice of homosexuality is incompatible with Christian teaching, self-avowed practicing homosexuals are not to be accepted as candidates, ordained as ministers, or appointed to serve in The United Methodist Church.

Finally, paragraph 332.6 states:

Ceremonies that celebrate homosexual unions shall not be conducted by our ministers and shall not be conducted in our churches.

It is this paragraph that led the Reverend Sally Haynes and the congregation at Trinity United Methodist Church in Kansas City, Missouri, to refuse to allow any more heterosexual weddings in their church until this part of our discipline was changed.

C. Proposals at General Conference: "We are not of one mind."

This coming week at General Conference, many of the proposals will seek to strike down the prohibitive and negative language you've just heard regarding homosexuality and replace it with phrases that recognize that our denomination is "not of one mind" on these issues. With the scriptural verses and church stance before us, let's look at why progressives in the church want to change our official position as a denomination on the issue of homosexuality.

I. Why Progressives Want to Change the Current United Methodist Stance

A. How They View the Bible

My friends who are progressives want to change the United Methodist position so that gays and lesbians who are devoted to Christ can be pastors, can marry persons of the same sex, and so that all pastors and United Methodist churches can, if they choose, offer same-sex unions.

They see this issue as a civil rights and justice issue. They champion this cause out of a sense of compassion and concern for homosexuals. While some progressives are radical liberals, you might be surprised to learn that many are not. Some are

They see this issue as a civil rights and justice issue. They champion this cause out of a sense of compassion and concern for homosexuals. While some progressives are radical liberals, you might be surprised to learn that many are not.

evangelical Christians in every way, believing people need Jesus Christ, holding to the inspiration of the Scriptures, and placing a strong emphasis on a personal relationship with Jesus Christ. Some of you would ask, "How is this possible? How could anyone believe both in the inspiration of the Scriptures and the acceptance of homosexual love and the ordination of homosexuals?" Let me take just a moment to answer this question.

First, while most progressives believe the Bible is inspired by the Holy Spirit, they also believe that the Spirit worked through human beings in writing the Scriptures—human beings who lived in particular cultures and times. The challenge, always, in reading the Scriptures, is to discern how the timeless Word of God is communicated through people whose understandings were bound to their time. In addition, our task is to understand what in the Scriptures God was saying to the people of the day in which the Scriptures were written, and what was meant to be timeless.

Regarding the two passages from Leviticus, they would note that there are many things in the Law that are no longer practiced by Christians—and many Old Testament practices that were allowed then, which we consider wrong today. No evangelical Christians believe in polygamy, or the right of a husband to have a concubine—but these were accepted practices of old. Likewise, there are other prohibitions in the same section of Leviticus that we do not believe apply to today, including this one: "Do not wear clothing woven of two kinds of

173

material" in Leviticus 19:19 or "Do not plant your field with two kinds of seed"—in the same verse. These laws were important in setting Israel apart from her neighbors, but they do not, according to the progressives, describe God's eternal will. They were a reflection of the culture and times in which they were written.

Regarding the two passages in Paul's epistles to the Corinthians and Timothy, it is noted that the Greek words used here could denote a kind of homosexual practice common in the Greco-Roman world in which adult men were in relationship with boys. Some would say then that Paul was condemning a certain kind of practice, not homosexuality in general, in these passages.

Finally, regarding Romans 1 where Paul speaks of persons worshiping idols and turning their backs on God, and God thus giving them over to depravity, he notes that some gave up their *natural* heterosexual drives and substituted them with unnatural homosexual drives. These persons would point out that Paul had no concept of sexual orientation, and that for a homosexually oriented person, homosexual acts are natural, not unnatural. Hence they believe Paul is condemning heterosexuals who pursue homosexual acts. *Others believe he is condemning here sexual acts conducted in the worship of the pagan idols.* If you read this passage again with this in mind it is easy to see why some could believe this.

B. *How They View Homosexuality*

My progressive friends view most homosexuality as an orientation, likely inborn, but also influenced by environment. They do not believe someone chooses to be homosexual, or that an individual can change this fact. My friends who hold this position believe that somewhere between 5 percent and 10 percent of the population find themselves emotionally and physically attracted to persons of the same sex the way the other 90 to 95 percent of the population find themselves attracted to the opposite sex. Some see this as a tragedy— a kind of disability in which the homosexual is forced to live in a world designed for heterosexuals. Other see it as a gift from God—that this, along with hetero-sexuality, is not to be de-spised, but instead is, if lived out in a monoga-mous, committed rela-tionship, a blessing.

> My progressive friends view most homosexuality as an orientation, likely inborn, but also influenced by environment. They do not believe someone chooses to be homosexual.

These note that the biblical authors could not have understood what we know about orientation—that a cer-tain percentage of the population begin feeling attracted to members of the same sex at a very early age, and thus the Bible doesn't really address this situation at all.

C. At Issue in the Debate

At issue, then, in this debate for progressives, is civil rights for a minority who have often experienced a living hell and who cannot change. These Christian progressives are fighting for full inclusion in the church on the part of homosexuals—in-clusion that includes the right to marry, the right to serve as pastors, and the right to not be told that one is "incompatible with Christian teaching." For progressives, justice is at stake here—justice and the love of God revealed in Jesus Christ. Some progressives even consider themselves evangelical, but they feel a great compassion toward homosexuals and they be-lieve that God's grace is sufficient to allow such persons to par-ticipate fully in the life of the church.

II. Why Traditionalists Want to Retain the Current United Methodist Stance

Before taking a look at how the traditionalists in The United Methodist Church see this issue, I want to say that most of the traditionalist pastors I know in our denomination are not mean-spirited, uncaring people. They abhor the Fred Phelpses of the world. They believe in civil rights for gays and lesbians, and genuinely want to make their churches welcome for all people. They have personally ministered with homosexuals, recognize the pain that has been inflicted upon them, and they don't believe in easy answers. Most believe that for a large number of homosexuals, sexual orientation is not a choice, but the result of a host of complex factors. These pastors are compassionate, concerned, and feel torn between their compassion and their understanding of the Bible and Christian theology. Let's take a look at how they view the biblical passages for a moment.

A. *How They View the Bible*

Traditionalists have a great concern that progressives may be "selling out" the gospel. They note that the role of the Law of Moses in the Old Testament is meant to teach and guide us—and that the passages related to homosexuality do just that. They help us know God's will. They note that nearly all of the rest of the Holiness Code in Leviticus we still observe—prohibitions against incest, commandments to help the poor, and a concern for justice. They believe these passages rightly help us understand that God's will is that human beings not engage in homosexual activity.

> [Traditionalists] note that nearly all of the rest of the Holiness Code in Leviticus we still observe—prohibitions against incest, commandments to help the poor, and a concern for justice. They believe these passages rightly help us understand that God's will is that human beings not engage in homosexual activity.

These traditionalists look at the passages in 1 Corinthians 6 and 1 Timothy 1, and while recognizing the Greek words could include a form of homosexuality in which adult men took advantage of boys, they feel this is not the only meaning of these words. They can be used of homosexuality in general.

The traditionalists look at the passage in Romans and believe it is clearly indicative of Paul's understanding that homosexual intimacy is unnatural and its practice represents an example of the brokenness in all of us. They would note that homosexuality is no worse than the other sins Paul mentions, and that all of us commit these sins. But they do want to recognize that homosexual practice is something to be overcome by the grace of Christ, not something to be affirmed as acceptable practice.

These folks would also point to Genesis 1 and 2 and other passages about marriage throughout the Bible as indicative of the fact that God created human beings "male and female" and intended us to complement each other. They believe that the Bible teaches that heterosexuality is God's design and order for creation.

> [Traditionalists] believe that the Bible teaches that heterosexuality is God's design and order for creation.

B. *How They View Homosexuality*

Traditionalists in The United Methodist Church do not necessarily believe that homosexuality is a choice—in fact, most I know believe just the opposite. They, too, believe that homosexual orientation is a result of a complex set of factors. They recognize that some homosexuals recall from the earliest age being different. Many homosexual males recall same-sex attraction beginning at puberty. Traditionalists believe, like their progressive friends, that homosexual drive and attraction is likely not the result of one thing, but a host of factors including prenatal hormonal levels, the environment in which one is raised, traumatic childhood experiences, and a host of other factors not yet understood.

They would say that there is no sin in being homosexual. The question, for traditionalists, is what one does with this orientation. And here traditionalists say there is a choice. They believe it is possible to resist pursuing this orientation—and that it is God's will that we do resist this desire for sexual intimacy with someone of the same sex. They would say that when God says that something is wrong, it is because he loves us and knows it has a likelihood of causing pain for many who pursue it.

Finally, the traditionalist would say that no one is made by God to be homosexual—it is, like so many other aspects of our humanity, something that happens. It is not God's doing. They would see homosexual orientation as little different than a host of other aspects of our humanity that are broken. We are all oriented toward doing things that are not God's will for us. Most of us know that we are oriented to be materialistic, to have a compulsion and drive to consume more and more and more until it makes us sick. But God calls us, with his help, to overcome this desire, or at least not to give in to it. This is a huge struggle for some. In addition, many of us know that we are oriented by nature to be self-absorbed—but God calls us to overcome this orientation and to serve others. Likewise, for those who are heterosexual, our orientation does not necessarily include monogamy—by nature we lust, we have desires and drives that are not appropriate for God's people to act

> They would see homosexual orientation as little different than a host of other aspects of our humanity that are broken. We are all oriented toward doing things that are not God's will for us.

upon—and so we struggle to redirect and to serve God in these areas. The traditionalist would see homosexual orientation in much the same way.

C. At Issue in the Debate

For those who support the traditional understanding of homosexuality within The United Methodist Church, what is at stake in this debate is the authority of the Bible. They note that the question we must ask as Christians is What is the will of God for my life? And they note that when God tells us something is not his will, it is not because he doesn't love us, but because he does, and wants to keep us from harm. In addition, the traditionalist says, "If we aren't to take the Bible seriously where it is very clear, in both Old and New Testaments, in its evaluation of something as sin, then when do we take the Bible seriously?"

For some of you in our congregation who are traditionalists, to even consider seeing this issue another way would be "selling out." It would feel, to you, that you had turned your back on God and on the Scriptures, and that you were affirming something clearly marked as sinful in the Scriptures.

III. The Human Dimension: Stories from Church of the Resurrection's Family

So far I have tried to summarize the major argument on both sides of this debate. I have not done full justice to either view—there are a multitude of nuances and arguments that can be made for each—but I have offered a very basic introduction to the debate.

All of this remains simply hypothetical until we consider actual cases of people who are homosexual. I have found that I can have wonderful ideals so long as I don't personally know anyone who is affected by them. But hearing people's stories tends to test our hypothesis and force us to modify our views.

179

As I read your e-mails this week, one of the interesting things I heard again and again was that some of you once believed one thing about homosexuality, but when you discovered your child, your sister or brother, or your friend was gay, your views changed. I will say that I wish I could make each of you read all of these letters and e-mails, and then formulate your opinion. Allow me to give you a few examples from each side of this debate.

One young man wrote:

> I accepted Jesus as my Savior around the age of 11. I can remember as I started approaching my teenage years wondering why I wasn't feeling an attraction to girls. I remember at the age of 13 realizing that I was attracted to guys. I remember immediately panicking and confusion setting in. I thought there is no way I am like this. I'm not like those people. . . . I couldn't accept myself, so I started to pray. I prayed many, many days in my bedroom to the point of tears, asking God to please make these feelings go away. I never could fully accept it and say the words, "I am gay." . . . So many prayers were said to try to change these feelings. I never got to the point of attempting suicide, but it crossed my mind several times over the years. I thought it would be much easier to just be dead than to actually deal with these feelings that I was having that were so wrong. My church, my Bible and even my God said these things were wrong. I remember getting so angry with God. . . . I remember just crying and yelling in my room and asking him why he would do this to me. It seemed like after that moment I began to finally listen to him and realized that this was the hand I had been dealt in life and I needed to start living how God intended me to live. . . . I tried to define myself as a Christian first and by so many other things beside my sexuality.

He went on to tell me that he and his partner had an "overwhelming desire to live for God. We are both Christians, and that defines who we are and how we deal with things . . . which brings me to my current struggle, Pastor Adam. How do I get involved in a church? Many church members think that who I am is a sin. . . . I know that some people will be cruel. All I want in life is to be seen as a Christian man that loves God with all his heart and soul. I want to serve him the best I can."

Another man told how he thought he was gay, and, because he felt rejection by Christians, he left the church altogether. He began dating and pursued life in the homosexual community. But something wasn't right. He notes: "There was a consistent feeling that emerged. After each date I had the feeling that this wasn't right. I could try to suppress the feeling, but it just kept coming back. . . . Finally, I left this life behind, learning I was not gay. I came back to the church and to God. But I am still living with the consequences and the turmoil from that period of time."

One homosexual couple with a child who are a part of the Church of the Resurrection wrote to say, "Since our first Saturday night visit to Church of the Resurrection (COR), all three of us have changed. We feel blessed to have found a church home." Their son has since graduated from high school and is in college, leading a Bible study. His faith is the driving force in his life. This person wrote, "We are very proud of him and his choices. If my partner and I had not felt accepted and welcomed at COR, we would all be in a different place today—especially our son. He is a devout Christian and leads his life with this guiding him. . . . You have been a significant influence in my partner and my lives and a gigantic influence in my son's. For this and all your work I thank you. You are always in our prayers."

Another was a woman who had been away from the church for years. She had recommitted her life to Christ and felt God's grace, and that she was called to no longer pursue lesbian relationships. She came to Church of the Resurrection because she felt loved and accepted here. She wrote, "I love God so much and long to do his will. I am tortured by loneliness, confusion and frustration. Thank you for your prayers and acceptance."

One woman touched my heart as she described the love she has for her daughter, who is a lesbian. She noted how, as a little girl, her daughter loved God, and that she was a remarkable child. But as a teen, when she began to feel attracted to other girls, she was left with the impression that church, and God, were not for her. The young woman left the church. For years now her mother has been praying for her to be free from her homosexual orientation, but this has not happened. This mother writes, "I am left with an unbearable heaviness in my heart, that people who want to love can't love the ones they fall in love with. That doesn't apply to [heterosexuals]. I can fall in love with any man from anywhere [but my daughter cannot fall in love with those she's attracted to]." She continues, "I turn to God. I beg him for help. I question why people are gay. I am sobbing now as I write to you." Then she writes, " 'Oh my God, my God, why have you forsaken her? Why God? Why?' I can scream and sob and nearly burst with emotional anger and resentment. . . . I get suicidal too. I beg God to make me the homosexual . . . and give her heterosexuality."

One mother wrote, "I have known for four years that my son is a homosexual. This doesn't make me love him any

One mother wrote, "I have known for four years that my son is a homosexual. This doesn't make me love him any less than I did. In fact, I love him more since I know the struggle he has gone through his whole life."

It struck me, when I read her words, that the love of a mother for her son may very well be a picture of the love of our heavenly Father for his children who are gay.

Conclusions: Where Do We Go from Here?

Four years ago a couple came to see me, as I was preparing to preach on the topic of homosexuality [that sermon can be found in my book, *Confronting the Controversies*]. I will never forget their visit. They had each been married before. Each had a son from a previous marriage. They each told me about their sons; they shared similar stories— boys who had each struggled with same-sex attraction as young teens. The sons were prayed over. They sought to change. They did not want to be gay, but this is what they were. And

My heart was heavy, and has been all week. The neat and tidy categories and black-and-white certainties that we all want seemed elusive to me. I got on my knees next to my bed, praying in the darkness, and said, "Lord, what would you say to these people?"

each, independent of the other, had taken his own life. These parents had eight by ten photographs in their hands of their sons and said, "When you preach on this issue, we want you to see our sons in your mind's eye."

At 1:45 A.M. this last Tuesday I finished reading these letters. My heart was heavy, and has been all week. The neat and tidy categories and black-and-white certainties that we all want seemed elusive to me. I got on my knees next to my bed, praying in the darkness, and said, "Lord, what would you say to these people? What would you say to those who want to be free of this struggle? What would you say to those who have found peace in living in their skin? What would you tell them about how you see this issue, Lord?"

But as I knelt there in the darkness there was only one idea that came to my mind—a Scripture passage from Paul's letter to the Corinthians, the thirteenth chapter, but not the verses you may be thinking of. It was the twelfth through the thirteenth verses where Paul writes:

> For now we see in a mirror, dimly, but then we will see face to face. Now I know only in part; then I will know fully, even as I have been fully known. And now faith, hope, and love abide, these three; and the greatest of these is love.

All week long, as I struggled to prepare *the* answer to the question of homosexuality, this was what kept running through my mind: We see through a mirror or glass dimly. I don't completely understand! I know the Bible—I have studied these verses as much as or more than most of you here. But when I listen to the stories, I find myself torn. I am not a progressive, and I am not a traditionalist. And I don't know the answer; I see through a glass dimly.

But these last words in this verse I think define my thinking about this issue. And now faith, hope, and love abide. Faith—this is trusting in Jesus as our Savior; trust in God, that he understands us, how we're wired, what we are and are not capable of. My task is not to completely understand sexual orientation; it is to invite you to trust in Christ, to allow God to love you. This faith becomes the center of our lives whether we are heterosexual or homosexual. It is what defines us. I am inviting you, regardless of who you are attracted to, to see yourself as clay placed on God's potter's wheel, inviting him to make you into whatever he has in store for you to be.

Hope. This kind of faith produces hope—a hope that God will deliver us and save us from our failings, from our inability to see the truth, from our reading and misreading of Scripture, from our feelings of despair. God may be calling you to struggle in this life, but he promises you will not struggle forever. He promises that he will be with you in the struggle. I have hope that God will help us as the church to discern his will as we move forward. We have hope that God is good, and hope in his mercies and his love.

But then there is this last one, love. This is what I believe we're called to do here at Church of the Resurrection. I don't have all the answers. I am not comfortable setting aside the Scriptures, and I am not comfortable thinking they apply as woodenly as they once did. I cannot completely see what God wants our church to do in this area. But the one thing I can see clearly is that we are called to love. We are called to love people. And we will be a church that does this—that loves nonreligious and nominally religious people, that loves gay and straight people. We will be a church where people who struggle can know that they will be loved. If you are here today, and you are willing to attend church in a place where the congregation, or at least the pastor, is still struggling to understand, where we live in ambiguity and see through a glass dimly, where you will be challenged to trust in Christ, invite him to shape you, and where you will be loved, whether you are gay or straight, you are welcome here. Paul said that these three abide: "faith, hope, and love . . . and the greatest of these is love" (1 Corinthians 13:13).

A Postscript Several Years Later

A friend recently said of the issue of homosexuality: "There is some third option out there that no one has been able to articulate yet, that will help us all move forward." I think he's right. I find myself conflicted. I believe the Bible clearly teaches that God's design for marriage is heterosexuality and that there is something important about the male and female complementing each other, not simply physiologically, but also emotionally and spiritually. At the same time, I believe that there are those who do not fit the norm of Scripture. Whether the reason for this is genetic, biochemical, neurological, or a result of childhood experiences or other life experiences, these persons simply do not fit the profile of the 90 to 95 percent of the population who are attracted to persons of the opposite sex. And, as people who have often been pushed away from Christ and the church by religious people, I believe Jesus would reach out to them, and love them.

I find it disturbing that the church that was founded by Jesus has devoted so much of its time and energy in the last few years to leading efforts against certain rights for homosexuals. I can't imagine Jesus would be pleased. At the same time I am uncertain that Jesus would be so quick to set aside heterosexual marriage as the norm and ideal for marriage.

This is how I have resolved this issue (for now). First, I think in terms used by Leslie Weatherhead in his excellent little book *The Will of God*, where he spoke of God's ideal will, and God's circumstantial will. I believe heterosexual marriage between two people who love each other sacrificially and help each other grow in Christ is God's ideal will. Having counseled with hundreds of couples, I know that God's ideal will is not always realized, even in the context of heterosexual marriage. Weatherhead notes that there are circumstances in which God's ideal will is not accomplished— and in those circumstances, God has a will for our lives, a kind of "Plan B." Homosexuality would seem to be one of those "circumstances" that calls for God's "Plan B."

The second way I've brought some resolution to my inner struggle over the two sides of this issue is by thinking of my own daughters. I try to imagine if one of my daughters felt she was homosexual. How would I respond to her? I would love her. I would want her to be welcome in our church. Would I welcome her if she wanted to bring her partner to church? Would I be able to love the person she loved? I think I would.

Notes

1. Dr. Lewis Smedes was professor emeritus of Christian ethics and theology at Fuller Theological Seminary. This quotation is taken from his article "Like the Wideness of the Sea," which can be read at www.soulforce.org/article/638.
2. The percentage of the population who are gay or lesbian varies greatly depending upon the person reporting the data. The statistics range from around 1 percent to 10 percent. See the summary of various surveys listed in the article, "Demographics of Sexual Orientation" on the Wikipedia website found at http://en.wikipedia.org/wiki/Demographics_of_sexual_orientation for a wide range of survey data. Five percent seems to me, and to many in the media, to be a safe estimate.
3. I did not mention, in this sermon, two other passages from the Epistles that are sometimes lifted up in connection to homosexuality: 2 Peter 2:6-10 and Jude 7. I should have mentioned these. They do not specifically mention homosexuality, but they do refer to Sodom as an example of sexual immorality. Depending upon how one views the sin of Sodom—whether it was homosexual gang rape, or the love shared between two persons of the same sex—one will either see these two passages as referring to homosexuality, or not. Having said that, I think it not unlikely that the New Testament authors did believe homosexual intimacy was "immoral."

Twenty
The Questions of War

"You have heard that it was said, 'You shall love your neighbor
and hate your enemy.' But I say to you, Love your enemies and pray
for those who persecute you, so that you may be children of your
Father in heaven; for he makes his sun rise on the evil and on the good,
and sends rain on the righteous and on the unrighteous. For if you love
those who love you, what reward do you have? Do not even the tax
collectors do the same? And if you greet only your brothers and sisters,
what more are you doing than others? Do not even the Gentiles do
the same? Be perfect, therefore, as your heavenly Father is perfect."
—Matthew 5:43-48

In the months leading up to the war in Iraq I found myself increasing unsettled about the rhetoric and increasingly certain that our president was intent on leading us into war. I am no pacifist; I believe that there are times where war is necessary. But as I read, studied, and listened to both the rhetoric and the responses, this did not seem like one of those times. Yet 70 percent of the American public supported the idea of going to war. I tried to raise questions in sermons, though admittedly I was timid. I had preached on the issue a couple of times in the previous two years—a sermon on what constituted Just War three months before September 11, 2001, that seemed prescient in hindsight; two sermons following 9/11 calling for restraint in our response, lest we "pour fuel on a fire we have not understood, and multiply exponentially the numbers of Osama Bin Laden's followers." Again, on the anniversary of 9/11, I led our congregation to examine how the ethics of Jesus might shape our policies toward Iraq.

In February of 2003, a small peace demonstration was being held on a major intersection near our church, organized by several laywomen from another church. The demonstration would not be disrespectful to the president but would positively make a statement asking the president to not lead us into war. It was on a snowy Sunday right after church. I announced to our congregation that I would be there with my family and invited any who wished to join me to do so. A handful did. I was interviewed by the *Kansas City Star* and gave a brief comment on why I was there.

Some were angered that I would not be fully in support of our president. I received a handful of letters from people expressing their "disappointment" in me as their pastor. And at least a few families withdrew their membership from our church. Following this I wrote a paper for our congregation entitled "The Questions of War." What follows is that paper, published on the first of March, nineteen days before the United States invaded Iraq. My point in reproducing it here is not so much to cast judgment on our invasion of Iraq. We cannot go back and change the past. Rather, I hope to model how we might think about these issues, and the moral points to consider, as we look at future conflicts.

> I received a handful of letters from people expressing their "disappointment" in me as their pastor. And at least a few families withdrew their membership from our church.

The Questions of War

March 1, 2003
Introduction

I am writing this position paper as a means of raising what I believe to be important questions regarding the issues surrounding a war with Iraq. But raising the moral questions regarding war, in today's environment, sparks strong feelings on the part of many. Many in our nation consider it unpatriotic to question the president's position. Some who have family serving in the military perceive the questioning of the current policy toward Iraq as an affront to the men and women in uniform, and thus experience pain from such questions. Others fear a repeat of the Vietnam-era protests and the psychological wounds inflicted upon many of the soldiers from that conflict when they returned to the United States to find a nation sharply divided over the war.

Many in our nation have accepted the administration's case for the use of force in Iraq. They find the arguments compelling and can't understand why some would not find them so. They believe questioning the president's policy will undermine our efforts to defeat Saddam Hussein. What is needed now, they say, is unity, not criticism.

Finally, there are many who have rallied for peace in ways that showed disrespect for the president and for all who accept his position on the war. The actions and methods of these persons precipitate a strong reaction on the part of most Americans. I myself find some of the rhetoric on the part of the antiwar folks inappropriate and unhelpful.

Given these concerns, I am writing this paper to raise questions, both about the assumptions and perspectives I have just listed, and about the morality of the proposed use of force with Iraq. I offer these questions with respect and the recognition that the answers I offer could be wrong, and that more information could make it apparent that a preventative war is the only option and, in fact, the moral decision. With the information currently available, I have serious reservations about this conclusion and I believe it is the responsibility of churches and clergy to raise these questions.

I. Can One Support the Troops While Questioning the War?

A. Is it possible to be supportive of the men and women who are deployed in the military while raising questions regarding the morality of a preemptive war with Iraq?

191

I recognize the need for our soldiers to have both courage and determination as they go into battle. I do not wish to undermine this. If deployed by our commander-in-chief they must fulfill their duty. Serving in the military is an admirable vocation. I believe in the need for a strong military. I am not a pacifist. I believe the military is important to preserve peace and to protect our nation. I am praying daily for our troops, and I wish to support them fully. At Church of the Resurrection we have already held one special service of prayer for our men and women in the armed forces and we will offer more of these services in the months ahead. We have the names and photographs of our servicemen and servicewomen in our building with requests that our congregation pray for them regularly. I have nothing but the utmost respect and admiration for these men and women. I am grateful for them, for their courage and willingness to risk their lives to fight for our nation and for freedom and justice in our world.

At the same time, we are not a totalitarian nation; our military fights to protect our right to a democratic form of government in which ideas are debated in public, and in which the people of our nation play a key role in shaping our policies. It is essential that we are free to raise questions, especially on the morality of the use of war. It is incumbent upon the leaders of the administration to make the case, in the public forum, for the just use of war. This is particularly true in the case of a preemptive war—a war that we initiate and in which we have made the first

It is essential that we are free to raise questions, especially on the morality of the use of war. It is incumbent upon the leaders of the administration to make the case, in the public forum, for the just use of war. This is particularly true in the case of a preemptive war.

strike. Asking questions and expressing disagreement with the president's position are a means of vocalizing the reservations many have regarding the present course regarding Iraq. To be silent signifies concurrence with the administration's policies.

I personally know a number of men and women currently deployed. I love these persons. I am proud to be their pastor. I am grateful for their military service. I am praying for them daily. When they come home I will honor them and their efforts.

B. Doesn't your asking these questions and expressing your concerns violate the principle of the separation of church and state?

The principle of separation of church and state is meant to keep the state from establishing an official religion or supporting a religion. It has nothing to do with churches or clergy expressing opinions or concerns regarding moral decisions in the public and private sector. The church is called upon to be salt and light—to relate the implications of the gospel of Jesus Christ to the issues facing our world. This includes matters of war and peace, justice and injustice, and a host of other moral issues.

When it comes to controversial moral issues I have never tried to dictate what our congregation members should believe. But I have regularly raised questions and invited our members to reflect upon the relationship between the gospel and the issues of our time. I will continue to do this. Christians, and Christianity, are meant to influence and shape our culture.

Twice in the last eighteen months I have raised questions about the moral issues related to the U.S. response to Iraq. At the same time, outside of our church, I have raised these issues or expressed support for a peaceful and diplomatic solution to this conflict both by attending a peace rally and by serving as a part of a panel discussion on KCUR radio on the war. I always seek to express that my views are not necessarily those of the people of the church that I pastor. At the same time, the views I have expressed are generally those held by The United Methodist Council of Bishops and reflect the Social Principles of The United Methodist Church.

II. The President's Case for War with Iraq

I want to take a moment, before raising further questions, to state as clearly as I understand it, the president's case for a preemptive war in which the United States initiates armed conflict with Iraq.

The president has stated that he does not wish to attack Iraq. He has stated that this is a means of last resort. At the same time he believes that in the very near future the United States may ultimately need to attack Iraq. President Bush has stated that such an attack is justified and necessary for the following reasons:

1. Iraq poses a security risk to the United States. A preemptive strike is necessary in order to protect our nation. This risk comes from the following:

a. Iraq may possess nuclear weapons, or may be seeking to develop them.

b. If Iraq did develop such weapons they might strike first against the United States.

c. Iraq has possessed chemical and biological weapons and it is believed that it still does possess some quantity of these weapons.

d. Iraq could use such weapons to strike the United States.

e. Iraq could give its nuclear, biological, or chemical weapons to terrorist organizations who would use them to strike the United States.

2. Iraq is a rogue nation, part of the "axis of evil" that threatens peace and stability in the Middle East. Iraq has repeatedly attacked its neighbors, including Iran and Kuwait.

3. The Iraqi regime has "gassed its own people," killing thousands of Kurdish Iraqis using chemical weapons. Saddam Hussein has oppressed his own people and they are hoping the United States will liberate them.

4. Iraq must be dealt with as a part of the American response to the attack upon our nation of September 11, 2001. It has been asserted that Iraq has links to Al Queda (also spelled Al Qui'da, Al Quaida, etc.), the terrorist network that masterminded this attack.

5. Iraq has not fully complied with the terms of the treaty that ended the Gulf War in 1991. The United States and Britain maintain that Iraq is in violation of this treaty and that it maintains a hidden arsenal of "weapons of mass destruction." If it will not comply voluntarily, it must be disarmed.

6. Failure to disarm Saddam Hussein would be akin to the appeasement policies of the European powers to Adolf Hitler in the 1930s—which ultimately were one of the greatest examples of the failure of this form of diplomacy. Our failure to disarm Hussein would create a true risk to the security not only of the United States, but the entire world.

These are the primary arguments, as I understand them, for why military action against Iraq must be used. Military action can be avoided if Saddam Hussein clearly proves that his administration has in fact destroyed all such weapons. In addition, the U.S. administration has, on several occasions, insisted that Saddam Hussein and his key leaders must also step down from their positions in the government—literal "regime change"—in order to avoid war. At other times, the president has seemed to back away from this position.

III. Questions about the Case for War

Before raising the questions regarding the just use of war, I would lift up the following questions regarding the administration's case for an attack on Iraq:

A. *Does Iraq truly pose a security threat to the United States?*

Senator Robert Byrd, the eighty-five-year-old senator from West Virginia, who has served in Congress for the last fifty years, summarized the feelings of many recently when he stated that Iraq is not a threat to United States security. This is a Third World country that would have absolutely nothing to gain by attacking the United States. Any kind of biological or chemical weapons attack on the United States would instantly justify war and would be met with the certain destruction of the Iraqi regime—an attack that would garner the support of the international community.

Providing weapons to terrorists would likewise justify immediate and swift reprisals on the part of the United States. There is no evidence that has been brought forward to date to indicate that terrorist attacks have utilized weapons provided by Iraq.

If Iraq did attack the United States or if Iraq knowingly supplied biological, chemical, or nuclear weapons to terrorists for use in attacks against the United States I would support the use of force against it. If it could be proved that Iraq had developed plans and intended to use its weapons in these ways, I would support a preemptive attack against it. To date neither of these assertions has been proved.

We do not need to live in fear of Iraq. This nation is no threat to the United States. We stood our ground against the Soviet Union, which had huge stockpiles of chemical, biological, and nuclear weapons, and delivery systems capable of reaching the United States. That nation was led by people not unlike Saddam Hussein. Peace was maintained through the threat of utter annihilation of both of our nations if either nation attacked (a policy known as MAD—Mutually Assured Destruction). In the case of Iraq, the overwhelming power of the United States would assure the destruction of that regime with minimal destruction to the United States. Again, Iraq is no threat to our national security.

B. Is Iraq a threat to her neighbors such that she must be dealt with by the United States to protect other nations in the region?

It is true that Iraq has invaded both Iran and Kuwait. The United States actually tacitly supported Iraq in its war with Iran, who was at that time considered to be a greater security risk to our nation. We rightly responded to Iraq's attack on Kuwait in 1991, defending this small nation and driving Iraqi troops back into its own borders. For the last twelve years Iraq has not attacked any of its other neighbors. If Iraq did attack any of its neighbors, the international community would support a war against Iraq as it did in 1991. Such a war would be justified as a response to an attack. I would support war on these terms.

During the last twelve years Iraq has not attacked its neighbors, nor does it show any signs of doing so at this time. Iraq seems to have been contained since the last Gulf War.

C. Does Iraq practice genocide against its own people, particularly the Kurds, and are the Iraqi people subject to oppression to a degree that justifies the United States invading and overthrowing the government of Iraq?

It is true that during one phase of a civil war within Iraq, the Iraqi military used chemical weapons against Kurdish Iraqis, killing several thousand persons. This is a clear violation of all moral and ethical standards and should have resulted in an international outcry and immediate response from the United States and the United Nations. Unfortunately, this incident occurred in 1988—*fifteen years ago*—and though the United States knew about this attack, we did little in response to it. I find it perplexing that this fifteen-year-old claim is brought up repeatedly as a justification for our attack of Iraq.

There is no doubt that the Iraqi regime has suppressed dissidents, assassinated persons who opposed Saddam Hussein, and put down rebellions with force. Russia and China, among other nations with whom we have friendly relations, have done the same. It is difficult to know how to respond to internal conflicts within a sovereign nation. The result is that other nations often do not become involved until it is too late. Witness our failure to stop the murder of hundreds of thousands of people in ethnic wars in Rwanda, Uganda, Bosnia, Cambodia, and a host of other places in the last thirty years. The current question, however, is whether Saddam Hussein is *presently* practicing genocide and the answer seems to be no. Again, the claim that he is "gassing his own people" stems from an incident fifteen years ago—one that should have been dealt with then.

I believe we were justified, along with Great Britain, in setting up the northern "no-fly zone" in Iraq to protect the Kurds from Iraqi aggression. Even this, however, is difficult to completely understand. We have, for years, flown military missions and retained some measure of control over large segments of Iraq via the northern and southern no-fly zones. There are a host of other nations—including Chechnya, the rebellious Russian republic, where far more blood has been shed by the Russians in trying to retain control over this region—in the world that would merit similar action, yet we would not consider setting up no-fly zones there, nor would we contemplate attacking Russia over its treatment of the people of Chechnya.

Regarding the oppression of the Iraqi people, there is no doubt that the Iraqi people have suffered in the last twelve years, in large part because of the United Nations' embargo pending Iraq's full compliance with the terms of the treaty of 1991. The Iraqis blame this oppression on the United States and other nations who support the embargo. We note that if Iraq would only fully comply with inspections and the destruction of weapons, the embargo would be lifted and the people would not live in poverty. It does seem likely to me that the Iraqi people are ready for the embargo to be over. It would also not surprise me to find them willing to embrace limited military action if it meant more food in the grocery stores. I am certain that many of the Iraqi people do not care for Saddam Hussein, that they are ready for the current threat of war to be over, and that they would welcome a lifting of the embargo. This is compelling, though unfortunately not a sufficient justification for war.

If Iraq were murdering significant numbers of its own citizens (not the occasional political murder—for as onerous as this is, it is never used as a justification for our attack on another country) as the Germans were doing in World War II, an attack for the purpose of liberation would be justified and I would support such a war. But there is insufficient evidence of current genocidal practices to justify an attack against Iraq.

D. Was Iraq in any way connected to the September 11, 2001, attacks against the United States?

If it could clearly be demonstrated that Iraq helped train the terrorists, as well as plan, support, and facilitate the terrorist attacks on the United States in September of 2001, this would have been an act of war against the United States and would clearly justify a military response. Assuming Iraq made no attempt at repentance and restitution, I would support the use of force against this nation to prevent further attacks and to bring about a just resolution. Yet to date there has been no evidence to link Iraq to the attack of 9/11. Prior to the last few months, Iraq has actually represented the very antithesis of what Osama Bin Laden and the Al Qaeda network stand for. Bin Laden has rejected secularized Muslim governments, seeking fundamentalist Islamic rule in Muslim and Arab nations. Saddam Hussein's government is a secular regime and Hussein himself would once have been the target of Bin Laden's disdain. Recently, Bin Laden has supported Hussein in response to America's threat to Iraq, but this is unusual. Attacking Iraq cannot be justified as a part of the response to 9/11; Iraq is not, and likely will never be, directly tied to this attack.

E. Has Iraq practiced intentional noncompliance with the treaty that ended the Gulf War? And if so, is a military strike, twelve years after this war, the only possible way to pressure Iraq to comply?

Iraq repeatedly has said that it has complied with the treaty that ended the Gulf War. It points to the weapons that were destroyed over the seven-year period of time following the Gulf War until inspectors left the country in 1998. It has said that it has no more nuclear weapons program, no more chemical and biological weapons program. It is difficult to understand why Iraq would not comply, if in fact it still has such weapons. Compliance would end the threat of war and bring relief from the embargo that is crippling this nation.

To date, the inspectors have found very little in the way of violations of the treaty. The Iraqis have, seemingly, cooperated with the UN weapons inspectors. The Bush administration claims that Iraq is not complying, but despite following up on every lead that our country has given the inspectors, no evidence of a continuing nuclear weapons program, nor the continuing production of biological or chemical weapons has been found. I do not know if the Iraqis are lying, as the Bush administration contends. It is possible, but if so, we must have some proof that they are lying. Once this is demonstrated the administration must determine what steps should be taken to disarm them. Up to this point the only significant violation of the treaty that I am aware of is its possession of the Al-Samood (also spelled Al-Samoud) missiles. Iraq is allowed by the terms of the treaty to possess missiles with a maximum range of 150 kilometers. The Al-Samood missiles, upon UN testing, were determined to have a range of 180 kilometers. These are now in the process of being destroyed.

Do we have sufficient proof to back up our claims that Iraq still possesses weapons of mass destruction? What would happen if we were to initiate war with Iraq only to find that there were, in fact, no weapons of mass destruction remaining in that country? Are we certain that the likelihood of Iraqi possession of such weapons, and their real threat to our nation and others, is worth the cost of military action? Does the risk of the possibility of the existence of certain quantities of these weapons justify the cost in human lives (thousands of military and civilian casualties) and in dollars (as much as $100 billion)? If the Iraqis do possess such weapons, is it possible that they are themselves embarrassed to admit their existence? Is there a way to privately open the door to their destruction? Are there any other incentives that can be used, either positively or negatively, to persuade the Iraqis to eliminate these weapons if they do exist? And is it possible that we are wrong and that these weapons have been destroyed? These are the lingering questions that cause me to reject, at this time, the use of force against Iraq based upon the argument of noncompliance.

F. Is Saddam Hussein a contemporary Hitler? Is a failure to overthrow his government by force akin to the appeasement of Hitler prior to World War II? Is the threat presented by Iraq similar to the threat presented by Germany during World War II?

It is clear that steps should have been taken to stop Adolf Hitler long before they were. Had there been a strong response to his aggression and atrocities, World War II might have been avoided. Upon learning of Hitler's "final solution," something should have been done to stop him. Once he in essence annexed Austria and large parts of Czechoslovakia, he should have been swiftly and seriously dealt with.[1] Instead, other nations appeased him and looked the other way. But was the situation in Germany leading up to World War II truly parallel to Iraq? I cannot see this. Germany was an industrialized country that built up a war machine capable of overrunning nearly all of Europe. Iraq was defeated in days by relatively modest fighting after it overran its tiny neighbor, Kuwait. Iraq is a Third World country with virtually no ability to threaten its neighbors. Hussein, for the last twelve years, has been contained. He is not currently practicing genocide against his own people, nor is he attacking his neighbors. I cannot see how we are currently appeasing Iraq, nor how Iraq is a threat to either the United States or its neighbors. Were it to take any aggressive action against its neighbors, or the United States, a war would be justified, would have international support, and would result in the swift end of the Hussein regime.

IV. Christian Just War Theory

Christians have wrestled over the last two thousand years with reconciling the teachings of Jesus with the idea of war. Many have seen in Jesus' teachings the basis for holding a pacifist position—a position maintaining that war is never justified, that there are always alternatives to war, and that it is never morally justified to kill another human being. Jesus' teaching regarding one's enemies—that we are to "turn the other cheek" when struck and that we are to "love your enemies" and "pray for those who persecute you"—were seen as the epitome of the pacifist position.

Yet the majority view within the Christian faith did not hold to this position. Christians noted that there were soldiers whom Jesus ministered to and he never commanded them to leave the military. Likewise, when Jesus was preparing his disciples for their work in the world after his departure he commanded them to take a sword with them (for self-defense). Christians accepted Jesus' words to "turn the other cheek" as the ideal for how individual Christians were to respond when they were slighted or wounded. But they asked this question: "If someone is hurting my neighbor, what is the loving thing to do?" It was felt by many that the loving thing to do, in that case, was to stop the perpetrator from hurting the innocent neighbor. It is not loving to pray for *someone else's* enemies while the other person is being tortured or killed. The loving thing, these Christians believed, was to stop the violence and torture—with force if necessary. This is the essence of Just War theory.

As it developed through the centuries, the Just War theory came to have five generally accepted conditions that must be met in order for a cause to justify the use of war, and two additional conditions for how war is to be fought justly. I will attempt to summarize these seven conditions and I invite the reader to consider whether the current crisis meets these criteria:

As it developed through the centuries, the Just War theory came to have five generally accepted conditions that must be met in order for a cause to justify the use of war, and two additional conditions for how war is to be fought justly.

1. *Just Cause:* This can be subjective. If our aim in going to war with Iraq is to protect innocent people, and if the threat from Iraq is in fact imminent and credible, or if Iraq has in fact participated in the terrorist attacks against the United States, or if Iraq is currently killing innocent people, then the cause may be just. If, as suggested above, these are not the case, it is possible that the cause is not just.

2. *Lawful Authority:* This is the idea that war must be waged by the legitimate authority of a people. Since, in our case, the president is our lawful authority, this requirement of just war theory is satisfied.

3. *Just Intent:* Our intent in fighting this war cannot be revenge, pride, acquiring control of oil, or for some personal gain. It is difficult to know what exactly influences individuals to pursue war, but I assume the best of our president and leaders and believe their intentions are right and that this criterion is satisfied.

4. *Last Resort:* This criterion, accepted since the seventeenth century by most Just War theorists, points to the need to pursue all other means possible for resolving conflict before war is used. The president would say that he has tried all other means. I don't believe this criterion has been met. What troubles me is that there seems to have been very little direct contact between high-ranking members of the Bush administration and the Iraqi regime. In conflict situations, face-to-face conversations with mediators present to guide the discussions often brings about positive results. In addition, the current efforts at containment seem, over the last twelve years, to have been generally successful.

5. *Reasonable Hope of Success:* This is both a pragmatic and a philosophical issue. First, is the war "winnable"? And second, will the act of going to war result in the ends for which war was waged? In the case of Iraq it is likely that we can defeat Iraq and bring "regime change." The greater question may be "Will the Middle East be a safer place, and will there be less danger

to the United States after this war?" I'll raise this question in more detail below.

Finally, there are two criteria in Just War theory that regulate how wars are to be fought if the war has in fact met the first five criteria:

6. *Discrimination:* This specifically refers to the agreement that noncombatants (civilians) are not legitimate military targets and hence that their deaths are to be avoided at all costs. It will be a challenge to see how Baghdad can be captured without a significant number of civilian casualties. It is clear that our military plans to do everything possible to minimize the number of deaths, but urban warfare will result in losses numbering probably in the thousands.

7. *Proportionality* (amount and type of force used): The force used to wage war, and the resulting death and destruction, should be in proportion to the harm done by the opponent or the threat of harm that it might render. In the war in Afghanistan there were over three thousand civilian deaths in the first year of this conflict. It seems likely that a similar number of civilian deaths would result in our war with Iraq. In addition, the U.S. government estimates the cost of rebuilding Iraq after the war to be $900 million. Does the wrong done by Iraq in a possible failure to disclose and destroy all weapons merit the death of three thousand civilians and $900 million in material destruction? Is the danger posed by the Iraqi regime's failure to do these things proportionate to these costs?

Not part of Just War theory, but pragmatically speaking, how much is it worth to the United States to see a regime change in Iraq when Saddam Hussein is already seventy years old (according to intelligence estimates; I believe he officially says

How much is it worth to the United States to see a regime change in Iraq?

he is sixty-five)? How much is it worth for us to be sure that Iraq really does not have any biological or chemical weapons? Is it worth one thousand soldiers' lives? Ten thousand? Is it worth the $100 billion price tag?[2]

The answer to these questions hinges on the answers to the earlier questions regarding the true threat of Iraq to U.S. security.

V. One Final Question

The last criterion for when one would wage a just war is knowing the war will have a reasonable chance of success. I want to close with one final question related to this criterion. Will our attack and destruction of Saddam Hussein's regime actually make the world, and particularly the United States, safer? Since the real threat to American security right now is not Iraq, but fundamentalist Muslim terrorists, I would ask the question this way: "Will our waging war with Iraq increase or decrease the likelihood of further terrorist attacks against the United States by Muslim extremists?"

Muslim extremists believe that the United States is the aggressor, is attacking Islam, is evil, and that, because Muslim governments are powerless against the United States, terrorist attacks against the United States are the only vehicle for effectively waging war against our nation. The perception in Arab nations is that Iraq has no weapons of mass destruction, is bending over backward to comply with the weapons inspectors, and that even U.S. allies believe this is an unjust war. In the light of this, an unprovoked invasion of Iraq, the death of thousands of civilians, and the overthrow of a Muslim regime seem to me to play into the paranoia and hate that inspires young men and women to sacrifice their own lives to inflict harm on the United States.

This by itself is not a reason to avoid going to war. If the cause were clearly just, if the danger to others from Iraq was clear and present, if Iraq's government had clearly been party to the attack on the United States, and if the international community was in agreement regarding the need for military force to be brought to bear against Iraq, the United States would need to step forward with military action knowing this was the only choice. But if these criteria are not met, and through our actions we created a more fertile ground for terrorism, we would have made a serious mistake that might take years to undo.

Conclusion

There is a part of me that could very easily support this war with Iraq. I don't like Saddam Hussein. I believe his arrogance has brought suffering to his own people. I believe Iraq might be a safer place without him (the challenge, as our own government is now acknowledging, will lay in what regime replaces him), and there is a part of me that still wants to seek revenge on Muslim nations for the attack made on the United States on September 11, 2001. I can understand why so many in our country support the president in this war, for there is a part of me that wants this war too.

At the same time, there is another part of me that, when I consider the questions raised above and the faith I profess in Jesus Christ, cannot justify a war in which our nation is the aggressor, particularly when there is not a clear and imminent threat. I grieve that the most Christian nation on the face of this planet, led by a president who is very vocal about his Christian faith, would attack a nation that is not currently threatening us, nor will ever be a serious threat to us.

While almost 70 percent of the U.S. population supports this war, The United Methodist Council of Bishops, the Roman Catholic Bishops, and a large number of other religious bodies have expressed their feelings that this war is not morally justified. I had supper this week with a retired army officer. He saw multiple tours of duty in Vietnam and was in the service for two decades. His son is now in the service deployed overseas. I believe his father before him was in the service. He captured the feelings I have had when he said, "Adam, I don't believe this war is right. It cannot be justified yet. I have fought in battle. I've been shot at. I am not afraid to fight and I believe there is a time for war. But I cannot see how this is that time." I spoke with the pastor of one of the largest conservative churches in our city. He said, "Adam, I supported Vietnam. I have never once thought about opposing or speaking out against a war—but for the first time in my life, I don't feel right about the course our nation is taking."

Over the last year the persons who have expressed their strongest support for me for the questions I have asked with regard to our approach to Iraq have been military personnel in our congregation. This is, of course, not true of all of them; we've certainly had military personnel who were upset by the questions I asked. But I have been surprised by the number of persons in our church who are in the military, or have been in the military, who have said to me, "I can't imagine that those people who are most supportive of going to war with Iraq have actually been in battle as I have. If they had, I can't believe they would so readily send our troops to war."

I believe there is "a time for war." At this juncture it is difficult to see that this is one of those times. I understand that thinking people will disagree about this. I do not propose that the position outlined above is the only position a Christian can hold. I raise these questions because I think they are important questions to wrestle with as we consider the path our nation is about to take.

I love our nation, and I care about our president. I pray twice daily for him. I am praying daily for Saddam Hussein, that God's Spirit will weigh heavily upon him to do the things that make for peace. Most especially, I pray for the men and women serving in the military, for God's Spirit to fill them with peace, courage, and hope, and that God might protect and keep them. I have written this paper to help those in our congregation understand more clearly why I have questioned the war effort, and why I have attempted to make a statement in favor of a peaceful and diplomatic solution to this current crisis.

A Postscript

I've included this paper to encourage readers to think carefully before embracing war as an instrument of foreign policy in the future. Christians, and particularly pastors, should help congregants think about the ethical dilemmas posed by war, and how we reconcile war with the teachings of Jesus. Many supported the war in Iraq when it began. A large number of these same people now consider the war a mistake. We cannot change the past. We must seek the most just resolution of this war, one that will bring a lasting peace. But we must also remember the events and outcomes of this war as we look to the future. I believe the "Bush Doctrine" regarding the use of preemptive war must be reevaluated in the light of the results of this war. This doctrine does not meet the criteria of Just War theory and it likely makes the world a much more dangerous place.

> I believe the "Bush Doctrine" regarding the use of preemptive war must be reevaluated in the light of the results of this war. This doctrine does not meet the criteria of Just War theory and it likely makes the world a much more dangerous place.

Notes

1. Britain and France did declare war on Germany immediately following the invasion of Poland. Although the major "shooting war" didn't start until Germany's invasion of France in the spring of 1940, hostilities did exist between the two sides as soon as the invasion of Poland took place.
2. As of December 6, 2007, the actual cost to date was $474 billion, and the estimates for the final cost of the war now are as high as $1.2 trillion. (See www.nationalpriorities.org/Cost-of-War/Cost-of-War-3.html for a running total of the cost of war to date). There have been close to four thousand U.S. troops who have died as a part of our war effort to date, and estimates for loss of Iraqi lives, both military and civilian, as a result of the war are difficult to determine. The Iraqi Body Count (IBC) website claims to calculate the total Iraqi deaths reported by the media, and its numbers, as of December 6, 2007, indicated a minimum of 77,922 Iraqi dead from the war and the violence that has erupted since Saddam Hussein was toppled. This would seem to be a conservative number; others have estimated numbers in the hundreds of thousands since the war began (for a current total, see www.iraqbodycount.org/).

Twenty-One
Faith and the Presidential Elections

> *Now the trumpet summons us again—not as a call to bear*
> *arms, though arms we need; not as a call to battle, though embat-*
> *tled we are—but a call to bear the burden of a long twilight strug-*
> *gle, year in and year out, "rejoicing in hope, patient in*
> *tribulation"—a struggle against the common enemies of man:*
> *tyranny, poverty, disease, and war itself. . . . With a good con-*
> *science our only sure reward, with history the final judge of our*
> *deeds, let us go forth to lead the land we love, asking His blessing*
> *and His help, but knowing that here on earth God's work must*
> *truly be our own.*
> —John F. Kennedy, First Inaugural Address

What role does *your* faith play in determining who you vote for for president of the United States? What role should a *candidate's* faith play in determining his or her fitness for office?

In the 2008 presidential primaries this issue came up in a variety of ways. There was an attempt by some in Internetland to label Barack Obama a Muslim (this despite the fact that he was baptized into the Christian faith in 1988 and has been a member of Trinity United Church of Christ ever since). There was the question of Mitt Romney's Mormonism and his faith. There was the question in one of the YouTube/CNN debates in which Joseph Dearing of Dallas, Texas, addressing the Republican presidential candidates, said, "How you answer this question will tell us everything we need to know about you." He then held up a Bible and asked, "Do you believe every word of this book?" Hillary Clinton and John Edwards, both United Methodists, spoke openly of how their faith in Christ sustained them through difficult trials. And

Mike Huckabee's rise in prominence was credited, in no small part, to his having been a Baptist pastor before entering politics.

A 2007 poll found that 60.7 percent of those with an opinion believed it important that the president be a religious individual, and the same poll found that roughly half of all respondents indicated that their personal religious faith "always or sometimes guides their political views."[1] Though the United States Constitution states, "no religious test shall ever be required as a qualification to any office or public trust under the United States,"[2] this only prohibits federal and state governments (and presumably local governments as well) from requiring persons holding public office to hold particular religious beliefs. This does not prohibit individual voters from taking a candidate's religious beliefs into account when making a decision about whom they will vote for.

> The Constitution's prohibition against a religious test for public office does not hinder individual voters from taking a candidate's religious beliefs into account when making a decision about whom they will vote for.

In fact, a candidate's religious beliefs, and more important, his or her practices, are very important for a voter to consider. My sense of this is based upon my own experience of how my faith affects the decisions I make and how I live my life.

Christians who take seriously the call of Jesus Christ on their lives seek to follow his teachings, to be led by the Spirit, and to hope to do Christ's will in everything. I urge the members of the congregation I pastor to take their faith into the workplace, to look at the business decisions they make, the way they manage their employees, and the work that they do through the lens of their faith. Likewise a serious Christian who was running for the presidency should do the same.

A president who is a Christian should seek to love God and neighbor, should long to "do justice, and to love kindness, / and to walk humbly with your God" (Micah 6:8), and should seek to do unto others as he or she would have them do unto themselves. A president who is a Christian should pray, seek wisdom from God, and be shaped by the values and teachings of the Bible. Such a person should be an individual of integrity, of honesty, of character—someone who puts the needs of others before their own.

But let's consider a few important questions we should ask as we think about the relationship between a candidate's faith and their qualifications for public office, particularly the presidency.

First, is the person earnestly a Christian, or has he or she become a Christian because it is politically expedient to do so? It is interesting to listen to candidates talk about their faith in today's political environment. All of the leading candidates for president in the 2008 primaries claimed to be followers of Jesus Christ. But I'm curious as to how many of them will still be followers of Christ after the election. The challenge, of course, is how to know whether someone's faith is earnest, or if he or she is simply using the language of faith to garner support. Do they have a personal faith? Do they pray? Read the Scriptures? Are they seeking to live a life worthy of the calling they have received? Do they worship regularly? Are they growing in love for God and neighbor? Do they seek to know God with their minds, love God with their hearts, and serve God with their hands? And do candidates exhibit, in any way, the fruit of the Spirit?

A second question is closely linked to the first: What *kind* or version of Christianity does the candidate embrace? Here it is helpful to remember that Adolf Hitler referred to himself publicly as a Christian, sprinkled references to God and to Christianity in his speeches, and yet, his version of Christianity was grossly different from what most of us would embrace.

I am personally looking for a candidate whose picture of Jesus Christ encompasses both the personal and social gospels. Does he or she know Christ personally *and,* at the same time, does he or she take seriously Jesus' teachings regarding peacemaking and the poor, humility and the hungry, doing unto others, and turning the other cheek? I'd like to know that the candidate takes seriously the Bible but also recognizes its complexity and is able to see the Scriptures in the light of their historical context. I'd love to vote for a candidate who was neither identified with the religious right or the religious left but someone who understood and could build a bridge between these two competing pictures of Christianity.

These issues were clearly seen in the 2004 presidential election. On the one hand, President Bush spoke freely and openly about his faith, yet many of his policies seemed inconsistent, to many Christians in the center and on the left, with words of Jesus in the gospels. It was frustrating to many of these Christians to have President Bush seen as the "values" president as though fighting against certain rights for homosexuals, appointing pro-life judges, and championing a war in Iraq were synonymous with, or the most important, "values" of Jesus. On the other hand, John Kerry, it seemed to many of them, was articulating important values that were consistent with Jesus, but he seemed distinctly uncomfortable talking about his faith—his words seemed forced, unnatural, and consequently disingenuous (I am not suggesting they were disingenuous, but simply that this is how his words came across to many Christians of the center and the left).

This leads to a third question: Is being a devout Christian enough to make one a great president? And a fourth question goes alongside the third: Can one be an excellent president and not be a devout Christian?

Is being a devout Christian enough to make one a great president? Can one be an excellent president and not be a devout Christian?

Regarding the third question—it clearly is not enough for one to be a devout Christian in order to be a capable president. There are a whole set of gifts needed by the leader of the most powerful nation on the face of the planet. One might be an earnest and serious

Christian but still lack the requisite intellectual, analytical, communication, diplomatic, ethical, political, and leadership gifts essential to lead the nation.

Here it is helpful to consider another situation: If someone you loved deeply was suffering from a brain tumor, would you choose a doctor based primarily upon his or her faith or would you look for someone who has extraordinary skills and experience working with patients suffering from this particular form of cancer? For me, I'm going with the doctor who is an expert in dealing with the particular type of cancer my loved one had. I would love that doctor to also be a Christian—one who would pray for my loved one and who would seek to be used by God to heal others. But if the doctor were not a believer, I would consider it part of my task to pray for him or her during the surgery.

In the same way, the skills needed to lead this nation, particularly on the international scene, are every bit as complex and important as those of a neurosurgeon. Given the choice between two equally gifted and experienced candidates for the presidency, each of whom might share my political views, one being a devout Christian, and one being an agnostic, I am voting for the Christian. The earnest Christian will be open to the work of the Spirit, will take seriously the teachings of Jesus, will find comfort and strength in prayer. But, if they were not equally gifted and the Christian lacked the gifts needed for this office while the non-Christian had remarkable gifts and shared more of my understanding of the issues, I would vote for the nonbeliever.

And this naturally leads to the final question: Can a non-Christian be an excellent president? Here I am reminded of evangelical scholar Mark Noll's comments about Abraham Lincoln:

> Lincoln never joined a church nor ever made a clear profession of standard Christian beliefs. . . . Lincoln's friend Jesse Fell noted that the president "seldom communicated to anyone his views" on religion, and he went on to suggest that those views were not orthodox: "on the innate depravity of man . . . the Atonement, the infallibility of the written revelation, the performance of miracles, the nature and design of . . . future rewards

and punishments . . . and many other subjects, he held opinions utterly at variance with what are usually taught in the church."[3]

Though Lincoln is often hailed as a hero of the religious right, Noll's assessment would suggest that were Lincoln running for office today, many in the religious right would be unlikely to vote for him!

Could Abraham Lincoln, with his unorthodox views on many Christian doctrines, be elected president today?

The times we live in require an extraordinary and gifted leader. It is not enough for the president to have a deep faith, as desirable as this is to me and to millions of others. He or she must possess the kind of diplomatic skills that will help rebuild bridges with other nations, while brokering peace between warring nations. The president must be capable of casting a vision for our nation in a number of important and strategic areas, and then inspire people to pursue that vision. He or she must be able to look at complex moral problems and find a way, with the help of advisors, for leading the nation forward. The president will need to lead the nation forward on issues like immigration, the environment, health care, and energy policy. I believe it is not an exaggeration to say that the future of our nation, and perhaps the world, will largely rest on the shoulders of the presidents we elect in the next twenty years.

When it comes to voting for president, bring your faith to bear on this decision. Pray and seek God's guidance. Watch the debates. Read as much as possible in order to be informed. See if you can discern if the candidates have a genuine faith or merely one of political convenience. If they are Christians, try to understand what their particular version of Christianity looks like. Listen carefully to their positions on key issues and evaluate their positions in the light of Scripture, tradition, experience, and reason.

I believe it is important to seek to discern which of the candidates have the leadership gifts necessary to preside over our nation. Which has great integrity, excellent communication skills, is intellectually capable, and has strong experience in leadership, in government, and can represent our nation well in foreign affairs. We must have a president who can restore our nation's credibility and respect in the international community. Finally, we need a president who can build bridges and bring people together in America. I believe that will require a candidate who is capable of seeing gray in a world of black and white.

Notes

1. "American Voters Want a Religious President" by Ethan Cole, *Christian Post Reporter*, June 15, 2007, found at www.christianpost.com/article/20070615/ 27995_Poll:__American_Voters_Want_a_Religious_President.htm. The poll was conducted by Sacred Heart University Polling Institute affiliated with Sacred Heart University.
2. Article VI, Section 3 of the U.S. Constitution.
3. Mark Noll, "The Ambiguous Religions of President Abraham Lincoln," *A History of Christianity in the United States and Canada* (Grand Rapids: Eerdman's, 1992). Noll is a professor at Wheaton College. This essay can be read at www.adherents.com/people/pl/Abraham_Lincoln.html.

Twenty-Two
A Worthy Vision for America

Grant us wisdom, grant us courage, . . .
Lest we miss thy kingdom's goal.
  —Harry Emerson Fosdick, *"God of Grace and God of Glory"*

Tim had grown up with money and had always gotten what he wanted. His first car was a special-edition Corvette. His parents bought it for him when he was fifteen. His dad was a wealthy and powerful man, and Tim knew it. When someone at school asked him to do something he didn't want to do, he would say, "Do you know who my dad is? He could get you fired just like that," and he'd snap his fingers. And often the person would back down. Tim had money, and he had power, and he thought quite a lot of himself. He expected that when, in a group, he proposed the group do something, everyone would go along with it. And usually they did. But the more self-absorbed Tim became, the less other people liked him. When Tim wrecked his new Corvette just after his sixteenth birthday, there were a lot of kids, and their parents, who felt just a bit of satisfaction. While some kids liked to be with Tim because he had great parties, took you on cool trips, and had the latest stuff to play with at his house, most people could only take so much of a teenager who always assumed that the world revolved around him.

In the global neighborhood, Tim is the United. We have 5 percent of the world's population and consume 22 percent of the total energy consumed each year.[1] We are about to give up the spot as the world's top producer of greenhouse gases to China, which may make us feel a bit better until we remember that China's population is four times larger than ours. We speak and

act and develop foreign policy as though we are the most important person at the table, and we do things expecting others to fall
in behind. We somehow believe it is our right to do unto others
what we want, not what we would have them do unto us. The
United States often seems, to other nations, self-absorbed, hypocritical, and unwilling to play by the rules. Our people struggle
with obesity, and we are known for our insatiable desire for more,
while thirty thousand people die every day in the Third World
from starvation and malnutrition-related diseases.

This is not how we see ourselves. We see ourselves as generous and willing to sacrifice to help others around the world who
are in need. We assume that a significant amount of our tax dollars goes to benefit other nations that are in need. We rightly remember and celebrate the amount of aid collected for the
Southeast Asia tsunami several years ago, as well as a host of other
international relief efforts that flow from the United States when
there is a crisis. We look at the millions of Americans every year
who participate in international mission trips to Third World
countries as evidence of our compassion. We see ourselves as the
champions of democracy, and the protector of free people around
the world.

So which image best fits us? The generous and selfless nation
that stands for the poor and oppressed and that pursues justice in
all that we do? Or are we the nation that is consumed with consuming? A nation that gives a relatively small part of our largesse
to help the world's poor? A nation that feels the world is ours to
command and that acts as though we are above the law? The truth
is that we're a bit of both.

Consider foreign aid, for example. According to the Congressional Research Service, in 2004, the United States was the largest
dollar donor in foreign aid in the entire world. But as a percentage of our gross domestic product (GDP)—of our wealth—we
ranked last among all developed nations, giving away .2 percent of
our GDP. This number has declined precipitously in the last fifty
years, in large part due to the end of the cold war. By comparison,
in the 1970s the number was five times as high. So while our in-

come has increased fivefold, the amount of dollars we give has actually decreased. We often think of our foreign aid as money sent to impoverished Third World countries. Half of our $20 billion in foreign aid in 2004 went to poverty initiatives and programs for poor nations. The other half, however, went to military aid and support to nations that are considered important to national security interests. Many are surprised to learn that our largest recipient of foreign aid is Israel.[2]

Imagine a man who is quite wealthy. His annual income is in excess of $1 million. He thinks himself generous because he gives away $2,000 per year to your church. The $2,000 is important and you are grateful for it. But the average member of your church makes $40,000 per year and gives nearly as much. When comparing apples to apples with the kind of humanitarian aid given by other nations (what is called "official development assistance" or ODA), Germany gives two times what the United States does in aid. France gives three times more of its GDP away. And Denmark donates seven times what the United States gives away.[3] But where the United States shines is not in official government expenditures in foreign aid, but in what individual Americans and nonprofit organizations give away in foreign assistance, most of which does go to those in need. In the year 2000 the U.S. Agency for International Development estimated that private aid given by Americans totaled $33.6 billion.[4]

We often think of our foreign aid as money sent to impoverished Third World countries. Half of our $20 billion in foreign aid in 2004 went to poverty initiatives and programs for poor nations. The other half, however, went to military aid and support to nations that are considered important to national security interests. Many are surprised to learn that our largest recipient of foreign aid is Israel.

This may explain why many in other nations say that they like Americans, just not the United States.

Christians should not be afraid to raise questions about our country's policies, or to challenge it to live more fully into its vision. At times when someone is critical of the United States, it seems that the most incensed people are Christians. "America, love it or leave it!" is the cry of some Christians who find it offensive to hear others point out our flaws.

But if any group should be both aware of our shortcomings and understand the reasons for them, it should be Christians. Part of what I appreciate about the Christian gospel is that it paints a realistic picture of the human condition. Christians believe that human beings were created in the image of God, but that image has been marred by sin. We each struggle with sin. As a nation of sinners, our nation will struggle with sin. Sin manifests itself in pride, self-absorption, violence, injustice, and a myriad of other ways. The Apostle Paul captured not only his struggle but also, I believe, our struggle as a nation, when he wrote:

> We all struggle with sin. If that is true of us as individuals, it will be true of our nation.

> I do not understand my own actions. For I do not do what I want, but I do the very thing I hate. . . . For I do not do the good I want, but the evil I do not want is what I do. Now if I do what I do not want, it is no longer I that do it, but sin that dwells within me.
>
> So I find it to be a law that when I want to do what is good, evil lies close at hand. For I delight in the law of God in my inmost self, but I see in my members another law at war with the law of my mind, making me captive to the law of sin that dwells in my members. Wretched man that I am! Who will rescue me from this body of death? (Romans 7:15, 19-24)

We all struggle with sin. If that is true of us as individuals, it will be true of our nation. And the nature of sin is that it often masks itself, and pretends that it is really good and not evil. Sin is easily rationalized, justified, and accepted as good.

Part of the role of the Christian community is to be a kind of conscience or guide to our nation—to gently, and sometimes not so gently, remind us of our ideals as a nation, and to say, "This path may not be consistent with our ideals as a nation, nor consistent with what is just and right." It is not unpatriotic to do this. It is not unpatriotic to call us to remember who we are as a nation, and to call us to pursue the highest ideals that nations can pursue.

> Part of the role of the Christian community is to be a kind of conscience or guide to our nation——to gently, and sometimes not so gently, remind us of our ideals as a nation, and to say, "This path may not be consistent with our ideals as a nation, nor consistent with what is just and right." It is not unpatriotic to do this.

When I think of what America can be I think of God's covenant with Abraham, when God said to Abraham:

> Now the LORD said to Abram, "Go from your country and your kindred and your father's house to the land that I will show you. I will make of you a great nation, and I will bless you, and make your name great, so that you will be a blessing. I will bless those who bless you, and the one who curses you I will curse; and in you *all the families of the earth shall be blessed.*" (Genesis 12:1-3, emphasis added)

What would happen if, as a nation, we owned the vision that God had blessed us so that we might be a blessing to other nations? I think we believe that about ourselves but, I wonder, does it actually guide our foreign policy? Does it shape how we allocate our federal budget?

When I think of what the United States could be I think of the words of Jesus:

223

"You are the salt of the earth; but if salt has lost its taste, how can its saltiness be restored? It is no longer good for anything, but is thrown out and trampled under foot.

"You are the light of the world. A city built on a hill cannot be hid. No one after lighting a lamp puts it under the bushel basket, but on the lampstand, and it gives light to all in the house. In the same way, let your light shine before others, so that they may see your good works and give glory to your Father in heaven." (Matthew 5:13-16)

Jesus felt compelled to mention, in this passage, that there is a real possibility that his followers might become tasteless salt, or that they might hide their light under a bushel. I fear that the rest of the world is finding America to be salt in name only, and that too often our light has been hidden under a bushel.

I am grateful that Jesus went on to demonstrate to his disciples what true greatness looks like, when, at the Last Supper, he took a basin of water, got down on his knees, and washed his disciples' feet, modeling for them what he had already taught them:

"You know that the rulers of the Gentiles lord it over them, and their great ones are tyrants over them. It will not be so among you; but whoever wishes to be great among you must be your servant, and whoever wishes to be first among you must be your slave; just as the Son of Man came not to be served but to serve, and to give his life a ransom for many." (Matthew 20:25-28)

The safety and security of our own country hinges on America's ability to reclaim our vision of being a light to the world, seeking to bless others, and carrying our power with humility. If we do not reclaim these attitudes, resentment of the United States by those abroad will continue to grow. Our "war on terror" will only exacerbate, rather than eliminate, the feelings that give rise to terrorists who would attack us. The only hope for creating lasting peace is for the United States to claim the biblical ideals of blessing, compassion, humility, and servanthood as defining characteristics of our nation and our foreign policy.

John Kotter, who taught leadership at Harvard Business School for many years, described the role of a leader as (1) casting a compelling vision; (2) aligning the resources to accomplish this vision; and (3) motivating and inspiring people to do whatever is necessary to make the vision a reality.[5] Our greatest presidents and leaders cast great visions for our nation and inspired us to sacrifice in order to pursue these visions. We are in need of a vision, as a nation, that will call us to true greatness—defined not by how much we have but how much we give of ourselves to lift others out of poverty and despair; defined not by how many people we can coax to do what we want but how well we listen to the needs, opinions, and thoughts of others in forging a way forward; defined not by the fear inspired by our military might but the admiration inspired by our compassion and generosity.

We are in need of a vision, as a nation, that will call us to true greatness—defined not by how much we have but how much we give of ourselves to lift others out of poverty and despair; defined not by how many people we can coax to do what we want but how well we listen to the needs, opinions, and thoughts of others in forging a way forward; defined not by the fear inspired by our military might but the admiration inspired by our compassion and generosity.

As I write these words I'm reminded of the words of the Apostle Paul in Philippians 2. He wrote them as a challenge to individual Christians. They strike me as capturing God's heart for America, and as a great starting point for a new way forward:

> Do nothing from selfish ambition or conceit, but in humility regard others as better than yourselves. Let each of you look not

to your own interests, but to the interests of others. Let the same
mind be in you that was in Christ Jesus,
     who, though he was in the form of God,
         did not regard equality with God
         as something to be exploited,
     but emptied himself,
         taking the form of a slave. (Philippians 2:3-7)

America has such incredible potential to create a better, safer,
and more just world. The key, I believe, is found in claiming several fundamental biblical ideals: "Blessed to be a blessing," "the
light of the world," and demonstrating true greatness through humility and service—this, I believe, is a worthy vision for America.

Notes

1. This according to the Energy Information Administration (August 2005). See
   also "2004 U.S. Energy Consumption by Energy Source" as cited in the
   Wikipedia article "Energy Use in the United States."
2. Congressional Research Service Report for Congress, "Foreign Aid: An Introductory Overview of U.S. Programs and Policy," April 1, 2004, which can
   be found at www.fpc.state.gov/documents/organization/31987.pdf.
3. Ibid, CRS-20 looking at the ODA number as .13 percent of U.S. GDP. I believe this number takes out military expenditures.
4. *Foreign Aid and the National Interest: Promoting Freedom, Security, and Opportunity*, "Overview," U.S. Agency for International Development, 27.
5. See Kotter's book, *Leading Change* (Boston: Harvard Business School Press,
   1996).

Twenty-Three
The Radical Center

*The best thing about the radical middle perspective . . . is that
it's just beginning to be articulated, examined, refined. YOU can
still affect it. And in many different guises, it's emerging
everywhere.*
—Mark Satin

*Would to God that all party names and unscriptural phrases
and forms which have divided the Christian world were forgot and
that we might all agree to sit down together as humble loving disciples, and at the feet of our common master to hear his word, to
abide in his spirit and to transcribe his life in our own.*
—John Wesley

In the late 1950s and early 1960s mainline churches had reached
their zenith of influence, growth, and power in this country.[1]
They were the dominant voice in America. They played a key role
in politics. They helped elect presidents and leaders of both houses
of Congress. But their power and influence were not to last. Since
1964 mainline churches have declined precipitously.

The reasons for this decline are numerous. Among them were
a loss of spiritual vitality as mainline churches increasingly focused
on the social gospel without a concomitant effort to help parishioners grow in their personal relationship with God; an emphasis
on the intellect in worship, while neglecting the emotion and the
heart; a kind of "traditionalism" in worship that felt devoid of
meaning and relevance for many; a shift to the cultural, political,
and theological left in the seminaries without adequately preparing graduates to minister in a culture in which the pendulum was

swinging to the right; a time of social upheaval in the 1960s and early 1970s that left many in society yearning for absolutes and a clear, black-and-white faith; and (for all of these reasons and more) a failure to "connect" with younger generations.[2]

I believe that in many ways conservative Christianity is today where the mainline churches were in 1964. It has reached its zenith of growth, power, and influence. The movement helped elect politicians, claimed to represent American values, and successfully welcomed millions of Americans into its churches. But I believe these churches are likely to see their growth stalled, and then to watch a period of decline, unless they recognize the changes happening in society that will leave them increasingly disconnected from emerging generations.

One of the most obvious signs of this impending change is the change in political fortunes for conservatives after a period in which all three branches of government were in the hands of the conservative element of the Republican Party.[3] The rise of what is called the Emergent Church within Christianity is another sign that the winds of change are blowing. Many of the voices in the Emergent Church are former conservative Christians who no longer identify with Fundamentalism's approach or interpretations of the gospel but still maintain an evangelical faith.

> I believe that in many ways conservative Christianity is today where the mainline churches were in 1964.

I see it anecdotally in a host of places. One of the leading conservative seminaries in the United States has students and professors questioning the doctrine of inerrancy (while the school continues to officially embrace the doctrine). I hear it in the reaction of my friends who pastor large Southern Baptist churches as they express their frustration over the infighting and the narrowness of some in leadership in their convention. I heard it recently as I spoke with the pastor of a large Pentecostal church as he expressed the frustration of many of the younger pastors in his denomination—a denomination that saw dramatic growth in the twentieth century but that is, for the first time, facing a plateau and, in some places, beginning to experience a decline.

I sensed it in the passion of a young pastor who leads a relatively new nondenominational church. His background was in the charismatic movement. He recently led his congregation to carry signs in a crowded shopping area in Kansas City announcing that "God loves gay people." And, on this issue, I hear it when speaking with my teenage daughter's friends who attend more conservative churches, yet who reject their parents' views on homosexuality.

I see it in evangelical publishing giant Zondervan Press's publication of an inclusive-language edition of the *New International Version* of the Bible, despite the protests and boycotts of the old guard among conservatives in America. I hear it in the willingness of an increasing number of traditionally conservative churches to embrace women in leadership positions in the church, including female pastors.

I see it in the Evangelicals who are speaking out against global warming despite the fact that some leading conservatives dismiss global warming as a hoax. I hear it in the questions raised by some very thoughtful writers in the evangelical magazine *Christianity Today* concerning war, poverty, and AIDS. Many of these same articles could very well have been published in what has traditionally been the more left-leaning *Christian Century*.

> I see the change in the evangelicals who are speaking out against global warming despite the fact that some leading conservatives dismiss global warming as a hoax.

And I've seen it in the ministries of two of the leading evangelical megachurches in America: Willow Creek, led by pastor Bill Hybels, and Saddleback Church, led by Rick Warren. Both of these men have moved from a ministry focused almost exclusively on evangelism, to one that recognizes the call of Christ to care for those in need. Both men have taken seriously their role in leading their churches, and the churches they influence, to be concerned about the social gospel even while continuing their passionate pursuit of the evangelical gospel. These men, and the churches they have influenced, are beginning to resemble the best of the mainline tradition. This is what many of America's mainline churches represented in their inception—a passionate evangelistic zeal coupled with a belief that the gospel had to be lived in social ministry to a broken world.

My point is that there is a significant shift toward the center that is happening among young people and key thinkers and leaders in the evangelical world. I believe this shift is unstoppable despite the efforts of conservatives to arrest it. The right is moving toward the center, and those who are unwilling to embrace changes would do well to study the mainline churches in order to prepare themselves for a long period of decline.

> A significant shift toward the center is happening among young people and key thinkers and leaders in the evangelical world. I believe this shift is unstoppable despite the efforts of conservatives to arrest it.

But it is not only the right that is shifting toward the center; changes are being experienced on the left as well.

Mainline churches are expressing a renewed passion for evangelism. They are embracing forms of worship that speak not only to the intellect but also to the heart. There is a renewed emphasis on church planting. And there is a recognition in mainline seminaries of the importance of spiritual formation and the spiritual disciplines in the Christian life. Many mainline seminaries have once again embraced the importance of the "apostolic core" of the gospel and are preparing students to do apologetics in a post-Christian culture.

When I speak at various conferences across the country and I talk of the mainline vision of the gospel as both authentically evangelical and at the same time liberal in spirit, mainline people break out in applause. I meet pastors and lay leaders of mainline churches who are energized by an approach to the gospel that brings together the best of both the right and the left. They resonate with the idea of a Christianity of the center and they inherently know that the world is far more gray than black and white.

Mainline churches have teetered on the brink of division over both theological issues and, particularly, the issue of homosexuality. Yet there are signs that there is a renewed interest in holding these churches together. At the General Conference of The United Methodist Church in 2004 a proposal was discussed among some, and then leaked to the press, that would have allowed for the division of The United Methodist Church between conservatives and everyone else. But the response of the delegates to the conference was overwhelmingly to affirm that they wanted to hold the church together. And the only way to hold the two sides of mainline churches together is to acknowledge gray and to meet in the center.

There will always be Christians on the right and on the left, but there is an increasing number of Christians who are drawn to the center—Christians who are learning to appreciate what the other side brings to the table, who are humbly willing to learn from others, and who are able to say with the eighteenth-century John Wesley:

> Though we cannot think alike, may we not love alike? May we not be of one heart, though we are not of one opinion? Without all doubt, we may. Herein all the children of God may unite, notwithstanding these smaller differences.[4]

Some characterize the Christian center as middle-of-the-road or wishy-washy. It is neither. A word that many in the center have often used to describe themselves is "moderate." But I don't believe the Christian center is moderate either. What does it mean to take something in "moderation"? When we speak of eating

Some characterize the Christian center as middle of the road or wishy-washy. It is neither.

or drinking in moderation, we mean that people consume in smaller portions. But I don't want to take my faith in moderation, or encourage others to do this. I am not interested in this kind of tepid faith. I call the people of the congregation I serve to a radical faith in which they have offered themselves wholly to God, and in which they should be willing to take risks and live boldly and courageously for God.

Each morning I wake up and pray this 250-year-old prayer Wesley taught his preachers to pray:

> I am not my own but thine. Put me to what you will. Rank me with whom you will. Put me to doing or put me to suffering. Let me be employed by you or laid aside for you. Let me be exalted for you or brought low for you. Let me be full or let me be empty. Let me have all things or let me have nothing. I freely and heartily yield all things to thy power and disposal. And now, glorious and blessed God, Father, Son and Holy Spirit, you are mine, and I am yours. So be it. And this covenant which I have made on earth, let it be ratified in heaven. Amen.[5]

This is not moderate. This is a *radical* faith. It is radical in its pursuit of truth wherever it can be found. It is radical in its commitment to love. And it is radical in its desire to follow Jesus Christ no matter what the cost.

Some in the political and social realm are speaking of a third way between the left and the right as the "radical center" that is able to hold together the best of the right and the left, and which forges something more powerful and true, and, in the case of the faith, more authentically Christian, as a result.

The radical center within the Christian faith embraces the evangelical gospel that proclaims that human beings are wounded by sin and are in need of saving, and that Jesus Christ is God's antidote to our human condition. *And* it em-

The "radical center" holds together the best of the right and the left, and forges something more powerful, true, and authentically Christian as a result.

braces the social gospel that seeks to love our neighbor as we love ourselves, and recognizes the Christian's responsibility for addressing the great problems of poverty, oppression, racism, the environment, and war. The evangelical gospel without the social gospel is spiritual narcissism. The social gospel without the evangelical gospel remains afflicted by sin and holds, in the words of the Apostle Paul, "to the outward form of godliness but denying its power" (2 Timothy 3:5a). The radical center holds that the gospel is incomplete without both its evangelical and social witness.

The radical center holds a fundamental conviction that God is "gracious and merciful, slow to anger and abounding in steadfast love" (Psalm 145:8). God is not a small god, nor a God that acts unjustly, nor does what is evil. At the same time, it holds that God is holy, and calls us to holiness: "as he who called you is holy, be holy yourselves" (1 Peter 1:15). It recognizes that grace without holiness is what Bonhoeffer called "cheap grace." But it also recognizes that holiness without grace negates the gospel and reverts to legalism.

The radical center holds together a liberal spirit that is open-minded, searching for truth, generous, and always reforming, with a conserving spirit that is unwilling to discard historic truths simply because they are historic. It is willing to question anything but requires a very high level of evidence before setting aside what has been treasured as truth by previous generations.

The radical center recognizes in the Scriptures both the reflections of human beings as they wrote of their faith, and the self-disclosure of God to his people. It studies the Scriptures critically, analyzing the historical context, the various situations that led the authors to write the biblical texts and the complex ways in which the biblical text came together. It is unafraid to admit that the Bible has challenging passages that likely reflect the theological worldview of its authors more than the nature and character of God who came to us in Jesus Christ. And yet, the radical center recognizes the Bible is our anchor, through which God has revealed himself, and in which God converses with us. The radical center sees the Bible as the history of a people who have sought to walk with God, and their theological insights and reflections. And yet the radical center also sees the Bible as a form of sacrament through which God's Spirit speaks and God's grace is poured into our lives. It is read, studied, memorized, meditated upon, but not worshiped or mindlessly followed.

The radical center holds that God gave us both an intellect and a heart and that both are essential to our faith. We can experience and know God with our hearts, and this personal knowledge of God is utterly life transforming and is the source of our spiritual comfort, joy, and hope. At the same time, God gave us the capacity to reason and think and ask questions, and God expects us to engage our minds in our pursuit of faith. We don't "check our brains at the door" to the church. Furthermore, we recognize that scientists, whether they recognize it or not, are instruments of God's self-disclosure as well. As they help us see and understand the universe, they are helping us understand the God who created all things and sustains them by his power and will. Science is not antithetical to faith but a partner in understanding God and God's creation.

The radical center avoids lambasting either the right or the left, though those in the center may be attacked by both extremes. They will not be conservative enough for the conservatives, or liberal enough for the liberals. But two defining characteristics of the radical center will be a willingness to find

> The radical center seeks to build bridges rather than walls and refuses to be the wedge in anyone's theological or culture wars.

what is good and true in others, and a commitment to practicing love. The radical center will seek to take seriously the words of Paul who said, "Let no evil talk come out of your mouths, but only what is useful for building up, as there is need, so that your words may give grace to those who hear" (Ephesians 4:29).

A friend recently passed on to me the words of Lucretia Mott, written in the 1860s:

It is time that Christians were judged more by their likeness to Christ than their notions of Christ. Were this sentiment generally admitted we should not see such tenacious adherence to what men deem opinions and doctrines of Christ while at the same time, in every day practice, is exhibited anything but a likeness of Christ.[6]

Mott could have been writing about the contemporary church. But her personal sentiments reflect those of the radical center. The radical center seeks to build bridges rather than walls, and refuses to be the wedge in anyone's theological or culture wars.

I wonder if this radical center resonates with you? I'm not concerned with whether you agree with every single position I've staked out in this book. I'm certain that with time I will come to disagree with some of the things I've written here. But do you have this sense, deep down inside, that the world is not nearly so black and white as many would paint it, and that the greatest truth is found somewhere in the center? If so I want to encourage you to speak up, and let your voice be heard. Do so, not belligerently but firmly; not with arrogance, but with conviction and love.

I'd like to end this book where I began, reiterating these words from the closing paragraph of the introduction:

Christianity is in need of a new reformation. The Fundamentalism of the last century is waning. And the Liberalism of the last fifty years has jettisoned too much of the historic Christian gospel to take its place. Christianity's next reformation will strike a middle path between Jerry Falwell and John Shelby Spong. It will draw upon what is best in both Fundamentalism and Liberalism by holding together the evangelical and social gospels, by combining a love of Scripture with a willingness to see both its humanity as well as its divinity, and by coupling a passionate desire to follow Jesus Christ with a reclamation of his heart toward those whom religious people have often rejected. This reformation will be led by people who are able to see the gray in a world of black and white.

An Invitation

Interested in joining the discussion? Log on at www.seeing-gray.org where you can read Adam Hamilton's blog, offer your insights, and find other resources for people who see gray.

Notes

1. "Mainline" is a term that typically is used to distinguish the established mainstream Christian denominations that are generally considered more centrist to progressive among which are the United Methodist, Episcopal, Disciples of Christ, United Church of Christ, the Evangelical Lutheran Church, and some Presbyterian denominations, among others.
2. This is a very cursory assessment of what happened to precipitate decline in the mainline. There are many other factors. It is commonly noted that mainline churches slowed the rate at which they were starting new churches as evangelical churches put a greater focus on new church planting. Some have suggested that a more "liberal" orientation among mainline seminaries reduced the urgency for leading people to Christ. Some have even suggested the mainline embrace of birth control meant they were having fewer babies!
3. By 2006 President Bush's appointees to the Supreme Court gave it a conservative majority, alongside conservative control of Congress and the White House.
4. "Catholic Spirit," one of John Wesley's most famous sermons, first published by Wesley in 1755. This quote is from *The Works of John Wesley*, vol. 11, ed. Thomas Jackson (1872).
5. My slightly paraphrased version of the Covenant Prayer in the Wesleyan Tradition, which is found in *The United Methodist Hymnal* (Nashville: The United Methodist Publishing House, 1989), 607.
6. *Christian Believer: Knowing God with Heart and Mind, Readings* (Nashville: Abingdon, 1999), 215.

Questions for Reflection and Discussion

Introduction: Are Jerry Falwell and John Shelby Spong Our Only Options?

1. What about the current role of Christian faith in public affairs creates the most discomfort or frustration for you?

2. Who in your life embodies the kind of balanced, mature faith the author describes? In what way would you wish that others could be like this person?

1. Are You Liberal or Conservative?

1. Which of your beliefs would you define as conservative, and which would you say are liberal? Do your beliefs tend to lean in one direction more often than the other?

2. How often do you converse with people whose beliefs differ significantly from yours? Do you find such conversations uncomfortable, invigorating, or some of each?

2. Straining Gnats

1. Name some of the ways that Christians in your community "strain at gnats," focusing on minor points of disagreement while ignoring the genuine and important needs around them.

2. Are there beliefs that you consider absolutely essential to your Christian faith? What are they? In what ways has your understanding of these beliefs changed over the years?

3. "If You Can't Say Anything Nice . . ."

1. Why do we find it so easy to speak ill of political leaders when we disagree with them? What is the difference between valid

disagreement with a politician's viewpoint and destructive attack on her or his character?

2. What is the most helpful way to pray for those with whom we disagree?

4. Stage Five: Spiritual Maturity and Gray

1. What are the most important changes that have taken place in your life since you were a young adolescent? In what ways do you wish to grow more?

2. In which of Fowler's stages of faith would you place yourself?

3. Are there people in your life who have come to embrace a broader, less black-and-white view of the world? What brought about this change in their perspective?

5. Finding the Sweet Spot

1. Which, in your opinion, is the bigger problem: legalism or libertinism?

2. How do you know when you should bend the rules and when you should follow them strictly? What principles guide you as you steer a course between legalism and libertinism?

6. Shhh! Just Listen!

1. Can you relate a time when listening to another's beliefs brought about a significant change in your own thinking? What was the change?

7. Being Pentecostal without Losing Your Mind

1. Does the place where you worship offer opportunities for what the author calls "wild, untamable" spiritual experiences? How do you react to such experiences? What kind of worship service most feeds your soul?

2. Have you been through a time when, like Francis in the chapter's story, you've been unable to feel God's presence in your life? Do these times of spiritual dryness pass quickly, or do they last a long time?

3. Why do some Christians fear thinking about their faith? Why do some Christians fear an emotional experience of the faith?

8. The Battle over the Bible

1. What does it mean to say that the Bible is inspired? What role did God play in its writing?

2. What part does the Bible play in your life and in your faith?

3. What does it mean to say that the Bible is both a divine book and a human document?

9. The Galileo Affair

1. What does science have to offer Christian faith? How can Christian faith add to what we learn about the world from science?

10. Apes, Evolution, Adam and Eve

1. Is belief in evolution compatible with Christian faith? Why or why not?

2. Of the three theories described in this chapter that relate Christian faith to evolution—Creation Science, Intelligent Design, and theistic evolution—which comes closest to your perspective?

11. Is *Your* Jesus Too Small?

1. How would you answer Jesus' question, "Who do you say I am?"

2. If Jesus came to the churches in your community, what do you think he would have to say to them?

3. In your own experience of Christian faith, is the evangelical gospel or the social gospel more important?

12. Will There Be Hindus in Heaven?

1. If your Jewish, or Muslim, or Hindu friend asked if you think they are going to heaven, how would you answer?
2. Are there people you expect *not* to see in heaven? Who are they?

13. The Logic of Hell

1. Which, if any, of the traditional ideas about hell make you uncomfortable?
2. What are your own beliefs about hell? Is it a place of eternal torment? Could hell function in some way to reclaim lost souls for God?

14. Where Is God When Bad Things Happen?

1. If God is in control of all that happens in the world, does that mean that God causes human suffering?
2. How is God involved when natural disasters like hurricanes, earthquakes, and tornados take human lives?
3. Has the death of someone you loved ever caused you to question God's love? What answers were you able to find to your questions?

15. In Praise of Honest Doubt

1. When in your walk with God have you wrestled with doubt? Were there specific persons or books that helped you as you worked through your doubts?

16. The Messy Truth about Spirituality

1. Who are the "spiritual giants" you've turned to for inspiration and answers? What have you learned from them? What are the limitations of what they have to teach?

17. Situation Ethics and WWJD

1. How do you decide what is right and wrong? What principles in your life guide your choices between one course of action and another?

2. The author says that "we have numerous resources to help us live lives that would please God." Who do you turn to for moral guidance? What persons or resources help you live a life that pleases God and demonstrates love for other people?

18. Abortion: Finding Common Ground

1. How would you characterize your own position on abortion?

2. Do you believe that abortion is always wrong, regardless of the circumstance? Or do you believe that a woman's rights in this matter are absolute, with no restrictions placed on them? If neither of these statements describes your beliefs, then what are the gray areas in your own thinking on the issue?

19. Homosexuality at the Center

1. Has your own thinking about homosexuality changed over the years? If so, in what way? Why has it changed?

2. How do you approach the biblical passages on homosexuality that the author has discussed? Are they timeless truths, as relevant today as when they were written? Are they conditioned by their historical context, less applicable to our situation than to the one in which they arose?

20. The Questions of War

1. How do you decide whether a war is justifiable or not? What difference does your faith make when considering this question?

2. In your beliefs, can Christians support and participate in war? If so, under what circumstances?

21. Faith and the Presidential Elections

1. How important is it to you that the person you vote for as president is a Christian?
2. Would a candidate's membership in a particular religious group prevent or strongly discourage you from voting for him or her? If so, what religions or denominations would you put on that list?

22. A Worthy Vision for America

1. Should Christians be concerned about the way that other nations perceive America's role in the world? Why or why not?
2. What steps can people of faith take to make America a more compassionate and just presence in the world?

23. The Radical Center

1. What signs do you see that a radical center is arising in response to the polarization of American religious and political life?
2. What can you do to make this radical center a reality?

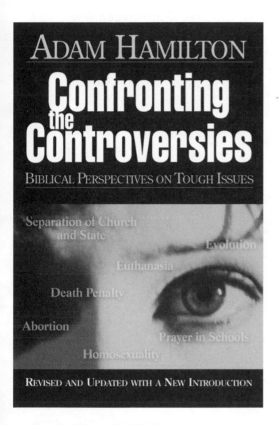

ADAM HAMILTON

Confronting
the
Controversies

BIBLICAL PERSPECTIVES ON TOUGH ISSUES

Separation of Church
and State

Evolution

Euthanasia

Death Penalty

Abortion

Prayer in Schools

Homosexuality

REVISED AND UPDATED WITH A NEW INTRODUCTION

"This is the sort of solid guidance on hard questions that Christians ought to expect from their pastors and their churches. Adam Hamilton faces the issues honestly and shares his conclusions openly."
—**Robin W. Lovin, Cary M. Maguire University Professor of Ethics, Perkins School of Theology**

"Among the great strengths of this volume is Adam's ability to hold positions in tension and to bridge the gaps that exist between people. . . . May this book become a model for us—that our own convictions may become stronger and deeper, even as we grow each day in our respect for others for whom God has not revealed wisdom in the same way."
—**Lovett H. Weems Jr., Distinguished Professor of Church Leadership, Director of the Lewis Center for Church Leadership, Wesley Theological Seminary**

In *Confronting the Controversies*, Adam Hamilton examines the issues of separation of church and state, prayer in public schools, euthanasia, the death penalty, abortion, homosexuality, and others.

Also available is a video-based small-group study on *Confronting the Controversies: Biblical Perspectives on Tough Issues*. For more information about this and other titles by Adam Hamilton, visit www.abingdonpress.com.

ISBN: 9780687346004

Abingdon Press

ADAM HAMILTON
Christianity
AND
World Religions
Wrestling with Questions People Ask

In *Christianity and World Religions*,
Adam Hamilton examines Hinduism,
Buddhism, Judaism, Islam and
Christianity, including points of
agreement with Christianity and points
of departure.

"In researching and writing
this book, I came to a deeper
appreciation of other religions.
I found myself inspired and
challenged by their teachings
and practices. I saw numerous
points of contact among the
faiths, as well as fundamental
and irreconcilable differences.
But this study, far from
weakening my faith, left me
with even stronger convictions
about the truth and power of
the Christian gospel."
—**Adam Hamilton**

Also available is a video-based
small-group study on
*Christianity and World
Religions*. For more
information about this and
other titles by Adam Hamilton,
visit www.abingdonpress.com.

ISBN: 9780687494309

 Abingdon Press

In *Christianity's Family Tree*, Adam Hamilton surveys eight different major Christian traditions including the Orthodox, Roman Catholic, Lutheran, Presbyterian, Episcopalian, Baptist, Pentecostal and Methodists, considering the history and distinctive emphases and practices of each. What do these churches share in common? Where do they differ? And what can you learn from each that will deepen your own faith?

Also available is a video-based small-group study on *Christianity's Family Tree: What Other Christians Believe and Why*. For more information about this and other titles by Adam Hamilton, visit www.abingdonpress.com.

ISBN: 9780687749116

More Praise for Seeing Gray in a World of Black and White

"Reverend Hamilton courageously addresses the challenging issues of our time prophetically as well as pastorally. A stimulating book, it is an excellent teaching tool for clergy and laity alike in addressing the contemporary burning issues of church and society. It opens much needed dialogue concerning various theological perspectives and strives toward the unity of the church."
—Sudarshana Devadhar, Resident Bishop New Jersey Area, The United Methodist Church

"*Seeing Gray in a World of Black and White* is a stream of refreshing water in a scorched desert of polarization! While the religious and political extremes compete for power and dominance through coercive rhetoric and power maneuvers, Adam Hamilton provides an alternative that is theologically grounded and faithful to the church's mission to be a sign and instrument of God's reconciliation in Jesus Christ. This is an important and timely call to the church!"
—Kenneth L. Carder, United Methodist Bishop, Ruth W. and A. Morris Williams, Jr. Professor of the Practice of Christian Ministry, Duke Divinity School

"The church and world have not been served well by either the Old Left or the New Right, who take partial truth and present it as the whole truth. Adam Hamilton provides a prophetic alternative voice to partisan advocates with their barren polarities and tiresome polemics."
—Lovett H. Weems, Jr., Distinguished Professor of Church Leadership and Director of the Lewis Center for Church Leadership, Wesley Theological Seminary, Washington, DC

"This is a wonderful book that is sure to yield some wonderful fruit as Adam's ideas are put into practice in the renewal of our church."
—Will Willimon, Resident Bishop, North Alabama Annual Conference, The United Methodist Church